PARADISE REGAINED

Prospects for a new
Social Order in the Third
Millennium

PARADISE REGAINED

Prospects for a new Social Order in the Third Millennium

By

Walter Prytulak

1stBooks - rev. 9/20/00

TABLE OF CONTENTS

NUTS AND BOLTS

INTODUCTION

Inalienable right to be free from hunger and malnutrition was proclaimed in the Universal Declaration on the Eradication of Hunger and Malnutrition adopted by the World Food Conference in 1974. It was reaffirmed and adopted by the World Food Summit at the level of Heads of State or Government held in Rome from 13 to 17 November 1996. The Director-General of the UN Food and Agriculture Organization (FAO), Dr. Jacques Diouf, in his opening speech called for a global action on hunger and malnutrition to ensure the fundamental human right to food.

This book does not attempt to solve the problem of world hunger to which one billion of people in the world are exposed. It is rather a proposal to solve the problem of the unimpeded access to food in wealthy countries like Canada or the United States, where only the minority of the population goes hungry, where food is aplenty, and where it could be remedied for a trifle and without the pains of labor. Thus, "Food for All" campaign is not disputed by anyone. As always, the devil is in the detail of how to implement it.

The proposal suggested in this book is that we give to ourselves Humanitarian Aid on a permanent basis as we do it now in any country in the world, stricken by a natural disaster. Such an aid would be financed by premiums, and would be more affordable, as it bypassed job creation and doling out borrowed or taxed away money. We should stop distributing money as if it grew on trees, and should instead feed the hungry with food, which at times grows despite us, and often needs tax money to suppress it.

This book was written in the firm conviction that the present socio-economic system cannot continue in its present form into the next millennium. It has been kept alive by hot and cold wars, by post-war reconstructions, public works programs, job creation at the expense of environment, built-in obsolescence, pressure sales and creative bookkeeping. These measures will not work in the 21st century. A full scale employment and world wars are out of the question. Our environment will not accept any further abuse and consumers will draw the line to their conspicuous consumption. Furthermore, the unemployed and hungry will destabilize the complacency of the well-to-do and of the sated in our society.

The free food staples, unconditionally accessible to all, with later addition of free shelter, health, education, clothing, and transportation plans, is at this time the only viable and detailed alternative for a social change in the next millennium that is being put on the table. The change, which it would bring about, would be from the present brand of capitalism, hamstrung by considerations for social welfare, to a society genuinely free from any ideology. There are no other proposals of substance on the table for such a change at the present time.

Headlines of the daily newspapers glare with the forecasts of gloom and doom: " World of work changing orbit," "*No one has found solutions* for tumult of current change," "We are in something that is going to change lives and the work that we do, and *no one has solutions,*" " When work disappears, has anyone got any better ideas than the hopelessly wrong-headed one of changing social behaviour by cutting welfare benefits?"

Of course, with eyes wide shut no solutions are in sight. The authors of the newspaper articles on the subject of work and procuring food for everyone in the society profoundly lack the ability of *lateral thinking.* It is as if they, and everyone else concerned about social issues, peered through a small hole in a kaleidoscope, representing our society, and each of them ascribed our social woes to the patterns they envisaged and the shards contained therein. However, from times immemorial, this social kaleidoscope has contained the same shards, which with each turn showed different image and a different pattern of color: money of all shades of green, printed, appropriated legally or illegally, taken from the rich, the old or the poor; different shades of private and public ownership, variable degrees of interest rates, big/small governments, state-owned/private enterprises, large/small social safety net, tax and spend/ cut and save, job creation, workfare and few others.

What is so disconcerting here is the fact that each of the visionaries hopes that giving this kaleidoscope a shake will change the essence of our society, knowing full well that, just as one cannot make a silk purse out of the sow's ear, shaking this kaleidoscope x-number of times, or adding a pinch of taxes on the rich here, or plenty of jobs-jobs-jobs there, will not transform it into anything else but only into a battered kaleidoscope, albeit bearing different political labels.

For what else but the fiddling with this social kaleidoscope would one call the following vision in which university researchers studied poverty up close and came up with a solution, that rather than go to food banks the hungry would be better off to grow their own produce (carrots) on the garden plots located beside a senior citizens' apartment buildings?

In another article "Pyramid projection indicates shape of jobless figures," a professor of economics at Dalhousie University computed that unemployed Canadians could have built 1.2 Khufu pyramids a year from 1990 to 1996 (given only hammer and chisels). Does anyone detect a strong musty odour to these shards?

It takes no more effort to gain a different perspective on things than to stop fiddling with this kaleidoscope, opening the other eye and then switching one's mental programming to that of lateral thinking. This accomplished, there would unfold itself a "promised land" in all its glory. After taking a long refreshing breath one would feel like saying: "Free at last!"

In this "promised land" there would be no welfare, workfare, or socially engineered compulsion to work (work ethic). The unbridled private enterprise would regain its long lost freedom to do what it knows best, i.e. to provide goods and services of high quality, most efficiently and at competitive prices. In this "promised land" private enterprise would at long last be able to shake off the government from its back and get out of the responsibility to provide social welfare to its workers. At long last it could disregard minimum wages, affirmative action and pay its employees variable retroactive wages, depending on the profit it realized. With the permission of its workforce, it would be free to 'exploit' it to its utmost in order to stay competitive. In this "promised land" everyone would regain *his/her freedom not to work* and refuse to be exploited, made possible by subscription to, and the introduction of the premium-supported Free Food Staples Plan. In this new social order such concepts as: job-creation, unemployment, social class distinction, labour strikes and panhandling, to mention just a few, would find themselves in a dustbin together with such other archaic concepts from the Middle Ages as strappado, incubi and succubi.

The content of this book centers on one hundred FAQ posed on my website for the past two years and the feedback that it brought about. These questions were raised and answered in National Issues Forum, conducted by The Globe & Mail, other network discussion groups on Internet, in e-mail addressed to me personally and in my informal discussions of this topic with those who were concerned.

I observed general inertia, inability, or lack of interest to think about new ways in which a society could be organized. It appeared that the majority of people felt more comfortable playing around with familiar concepts and worn out clichés, and sought a solution to our economic woes by constantly rearranging them. For a while I compared the minds of all the participants in this forum to the "black pitch-water," so colorfully described by H.W. Longfellow in the "Song of Hiawatha":

>"..........................Sluggish,
>Covered with its mould of ages,
>Black with rotting water-rushes,
>Rank with flags of leaves of lilies,
>Stagnant, lifeless, dreary, dismal..."

ADVANTAGES OF LIVING IN A SOCIETY

To understand why we do urgently need the availability of free food staples, we must consider the purpose of forming a society, the advantages of living in it, and the role of a government, as opposed to the unorganized existence in the wild.

To form a society and become civilized we had to give up our right of hunting, fishing, and each one of us owning, and tilling the land for our subsistence. We agreed that we would put out effort to get some food from a centrally located places and that only a few people would be involved in farming. We agreed to use money as a medium of exchange, and pay taxes, premiums, or prices to compensate them for their effort.

We live in an ideal mercenary society. The only requirement it imposes on us is that we pay our way. To buy anything we only need money, but not the proof that we had worked. Without money we cannot purchase anything. However, having paid the price for goods and services, we have no further obligation to the company or to the society that produced them, whether they are located in our own country or in faraway places in the world.

John F. Kennedy is often quoted as having said: "Ask not what your country can do for you but what you can do for your country." It is meaningful only in the society that is caring and which is run like a large family. In the mercenary society, on the other hand, one's obligation to the society is fully discharged by having paid his way for goods and services received. Besides having paid taxes, premiums and prices, what is this debt, which some people feel one still owes to his society? Is it something that money could *not* buy? Making additional sacrifices? And then, what would the society in question do to a person who refused to oblige? Would he be imprisoned? Starved? And what other means of enforcement would his society use to make him submit?

If the society does not care for the welfare of its subjects, after they have paid their way, why would they put out more effort to care for the welfare of their society? If a society survives by scavenging on the corpses of its members, than it should not be surprising when each member tries to survive by scavenging on the corpse of his society.

The main purpose of a society is to provide each of its members with a milieu in which humans could live in dignity, and to facilitate attainment, realization, and cultivation of such dignity.

Needless to say that individuals constituting a society and their elected government embodying and representing such a society, are mutually interdependent. Survival or death of one is tantamount to the survival or death of the other, as no individual could exist without his society and there would be no society without its individual members.

The Army may serve us as a paradigm of what a progressive, enlightened, and efficient civil society ought to be. A soldier in the army is provided for with respect to all of his needs. He does not have to buy his groceries, cook, or wash dishes. His underwear and uniforms are cleaned and pressed for him. His health, psychiatric, and dental needs are taken care of. Transportation and entertainment are provided for him free of charge. Why? Because, if he had to take care of all of his needs all by himself, he would have no time to perform his duties as a soldier. Just being a soldier guarantees for him all the above-mentioned benefits. He does not have to perform additional duties for the privilege of being a soldier. He is not asked whether he deserved his next meal by the number of enemies he killed or flushed out. Were things different, the army would totally disintegrate or become non-functional.

In a similar fashion in civil life, we are all soldiers without a uniform, building our society and creating an environment in which we could perform our chosen duties. It is of mutual self-interest to all of us to keep the society we live in healthy, to collectively take care of each other needs, in such a way that we would not be distracted from the task at hand. Without it we cannot be good soldiers in our civilian life, and without it the society is in danger of collapsing.

THE ROLE OF GOVERNMENT

Ideally then, the role of government, as a representative of all of us, should primarily be as follows: to see to it that its subjects were well fed, sheltered, healthy and safe. Secondly, to provide suitable environment for the new age living, to facilitate everyone who so chooses to move freely within the country, to be educated if so desired, to undertake any enterprise to manufacture, to create, to provide services, without bureaucratic impediments and the inconveniences of the wild. Further on, the role of government should be to help each individual to find justice under the Law, and to offer protection against unlawful and violent overtures by others.

I believe in a government:

that respects each individual's right to life, from the moment of his conception to the end of his natural span of life, i.e. a government which constitutionally guarantees food staples, free of charge to everyone, without strings attached;

a government that is not concerned with the size of my poverty or wealth and that does not worry about how I should occupy myself;

a government that abdicates its responsibility to create for me a job, and to dictate hiring practices, how long should my workday be, and how much should I earn per hour;

a government that does not push on me any ideology, or dictates to me how I should think, feel, and behave in my private life;

a government that does not restrict my style of life unless it interferes with that of others;

3

a government that keeps the shelves of the retail stores loaded with goods produced anywhere in the world; where the desire to acquire such goods constitutes the sole motivation to work; where the sweat of labour is not a virtue per se, but the unavoidable byproduct of an individual trying to reach a goal, set up by himself and for himself;

a government that regulates the circulation of money and controls monetary weather conditions in such a way that no part of the country becomes economically flooded or turned into a wasteland;

a government that enforces law and order, but does not exterminate criminals through capital punishment, and does not use any form of punishment to keep them on the path of righteousness;

and finally, a government that does not govern its people but rather facilitates them to govern themselves.

PRESENT SOCIO-ECONOMIC STRUCTURE

Our present economic system has survived only because of heroic measures undertaken to keep it alive in the absence of better alternatives. It has been on life support, subjected to leeching and bloodletting, to infusion of new capital, revival by shock, musical chairs played during the elections, and by pointing the accusing finger at the predecessor. By now it consists of layers upon layers of band-aids and bandages. It has been glued together by different social engineering experiments, by defensive armaments against evil empires, by countless wars, by frequent elections and the promise of change and better things to come, by pulling wool over the eyes of the electorate to keep them quiet, by deposing or murdering of hereditary rulers, by various social support systems, labour laws, human rights, constant fine-tuning of interest rates, job creating efforts, downsizing, mergers, subsidies, tax concessions, etc. Financial crises upon crises follow, requiring finance ministers of superpowers to huddle in attempt to rescue their respective economies. There is just no solution in sight. Tinkering with any aspect of it threatens the whole with a collapse. Everything under the sun has been already tried. It is like a house built of cards: remove one and the entire structure crumbles.

At present all free societies of the world leave the physical survival of an individual up to his own resources. It is up to him to forage for food, to find shelter, to find resources for becoming educated, and to seek medical treatment for his ills. In other words, man is considered to be the master of his own destiny. If he is homeless and starves or freezes to death while sleeping in the gutters, it is his own fault. He is branded lazy, irresponsible, a bum and a sloth that sponges on the productive work of others and therefore not deserving to receive help from his society. However, the selfsame individual may be called to serve in armed services in times of war, and be asked to make the ultimate sacrifice by giving up his life in defense of his country, which so sadly neglected him until then. It is not that people are free, but that governments are free of their obligation to their people.

Our present economic system is based on exploitation of our self-preservation instinct. Because we all want to survive we have to eat. However the access to the trough has been made difficult by the economic machine, and by the requirement that we have to compete with each other to reach it. We have to walk a long maze with many bends, and at each corner we have to push on heavy revolving door to get through. This is what the work ethic is about; if one wants to live one has to run the maze on a treadmill and naturally perform work as a byproduct. Thus wanting to live is exploited for productive ends. To increase productivity and profits, the maze has to be made more tortuous, the revolving doors heavier and the food in the trough scantier and harder to reach.

It may appear on the surface that government's main preoccupation is with helping everyone to live it up, to become rich, to lead a meaningful style of life, to drive a car, to surf the Internet, to attend cultural events, to live in a decent home, etc. In reality governments are preoccupied with less loftier goals, which are how to create jobs to provide people with money with which they could buy themselves enough food to live on. The chief cause of government's continual bite on our pocketbook is the financial impasse reached when it tries to feed people with money rather than with food.

In the former Soviet Union, a *universal employment scheme* was introduced, with government as a job-creator in the driver's seat. To my knowledge no private entrepreneur has ever been in such a business of job creation. To him job creation is like an unavoidable pollution, a necessary evil. Any private entrepreneur goes into business to create and manufacture goods of highest quality and to provide services, in a most efficient way, at lowest competitive cost, *without employing anyone*, if he can help it.

Job creation is a political term used by governments to refer to food provision for its subjects via 'honest' day's work. Because only governments are able to create jobs and are experts in it, the former Soviet Union embarked on this venture by creating large bureaucracy, massive military forces, vast social service industry and an army of undercover agents and informers. Famine was artificially created by requisitioning all food from the farmers in order to force them to give up their land and join the collectives, which they adamantly were refusing to do.

Following the example set by the former Soviet Union, unemployment could be instantaneously wiped out in the countries of the West: by increasing the size of the army and bureaucracy, and converting each person into an informer, working for the state. Thus to each would be given according to his needs, and everyone would have a few dollars with which to buy himself the staples to subsist on. Dictatorship would be the price, which one would have to pay.

Thus working for money in order to make living is not an idea concocted by the private enterprise but rather the one embraced by an ideological government. It was initially good for business, because it provided a captive pool of workers who had no choice but to work in order to survive. As things stand now, with downsizing, the free enterprise being more capital-intensive and less dependent on labour, governments have to rethink their food provision strategies: how to provide a source of livelihood for its workers, security in their old age, retirement income, sick and disability benefits, family leave, vacations, personal health, dental care, drug plan, safe working conditions, minimum wages etc., all of it without spending too much money on creating new jobs. Job sharing, shorter workweek, negative income tax, credits for community services, etc. are just a few possibilities for dealing with the problem. They are just band-aid treatments for a festering wound that refuses to heal.

The free enterprise is a goose that lays the golden egg and our sole preoccupation ought to be: to see to it that the goose is healthy, that the egg she lays is perfect, and that the laying of the egg does not injure her. It is government's responsibility to collect the goose's eggs and feed them to the people. However, if the goose is either too sick or unproductive, it ought to be governments' responsibility to find other sources of nourishment.

Governments are run in the family way, while businesses are run for profit. Governments cannot be businesslike because some things in a society have to be done for the good of the people, even if they bring no financial reward, even if they support some activities that are time and resource consuming and would result in bankruptcy if run for profit. On the other hand a business, run like a family, would go to pots. Put "society as a whole" in charge of, e.g. GM or Chrysler, and no cars would ever come out of the assembly line.

The marriage between the free enterprise and a government was not made in heaven. It is incompatible and unworkable for reasons that the goal of one is the profit, and of the other one is the good of the country. It is the union based on ideology of monogamous relationship in which it is the husband's duty to support his family. The following parable may illustrate this state of affairs more poignantly.

Canada, the young maiden, was pressed into marriage of convenience to an aggressive and wealthy entrepreneur. She proved to be obedient and subservient wife and he provided her with the necessities of life. For economic reasons he kept her busy, barefoot and pregnant in the kitchen. As a provider he usurped for himself the freedom to absent himself from time to time from home to discover new lands, to fight wars and to get involved in business transaction with other businesswomen.

Naturally wife was not very happy about this arrangement, but being a good woman divorce was not an option for her. She considered her marriage for better or for worse, until the death did them part. Eventually, with her help, her husband grew in his stature into a corporate giant. He began to object to having the obligation to support his wife and children on grounds that it took too great a bite out of his profits, which he though could be reinvested and bring about even greater profits. Then he started to default on his payments. When his wife made too many demands on him he would take off and enter common-law relationship with Taiwan, Singapore, Korea and others.

Everyone concerned was of the opinion that this marriage had to be saved at all costs and each side in the dispute hired counselors to help them reach some form of reconciliation.

Charles A. Reich, Ralph Nader, Noam Chomsky and others, to mention just a few, pointed their accusing finger at the husband's failing in his duties, his refusal to be involved in a marriage counseling, acting in an authoritarian way, not helping around the house, philandering, outsourcing his physical needs, trickling down too little money for his wife and their children's support, and having wild parties with her being excluded.

Marriage counselors concluded that husband was suffering from a personality disorder or was simply going through the male menopause. They recommended that he attend group psychotherapy sessions for wife abusers. The Court issued an order to pursue dead-beat dads wherever they happened to be, garnisheeing their wages and putting them in jail.

Taking the side of husband were members of Fortune 500 club, paid hacks, the like those of the Fraser Institute in Canada. Their arguments were typically male-oriented: The husband needed freedom to grow. The stimulation of extramarital relationships in faraway places was quintessential to his mental health. This made him more vigorous and more able to compete, so that he could better feed his wife. She, they said, was economically unproductive and, not being able to show even one pennyworth of profit for her efforts, could not subsist on just nothing without him. For their marriage to function, they said, she needed to change her attitudes, break the cycle of her dependence on him, become retrained, acquire new skills and become self-supporting. Above all, it was in her interest to remain quiet and not drive him away from marriage by her constant whining.

Wife protested. The running the family –she said -- is not the same as the running of the business. In business the bottom line determined whether the venture was viable or not, regardless of the family welfare. In the family its health, welfare and happiness came first regardless of the bottom line. In business the bottom line was the dictator, whereas in the family the head of the family dictates. Mother knows best.

In a family –she continued-- the personal profit was of no consequence. One did things out of sense of duty, out of love for other members of the family, or simply because one was

9

commanded to do it. Everybody pitched in. The chores were done in rotation. Private property was private until other members of the family had a pressing need to use it. The use of facilities, television, and telephone was shared and regimented. Free speech, freedom of association and of movement was severely curtailed for the good of the family. John F. Kennedy's dictum "Ask not what the country can do for you but what you can do for your country" had relevance only in such a family setting, because a country was nothing more than a large family. Had he business in mind, he would have said: "Ask not what your businesses can do for you, but what you can do for your businesses."

No resolution of the problem was possible until the expert in conjugal disharmony was consulted. His name was Prof. Free Foodstaples. This is   what he said to the couple:

I have been watching your constant wife-and-husband-bashing reaching at times murderous proportions. I said to myself:

> "Fiddle de dee, fiddle de dee,
> The fly has married the bumblebee.
> They went to the church and married was she,
> The fly has married the bumblebee."

There is nothing wrong with you wife, the domestic fly, or with your husband, the bumblebee. The problem is that as spouses you were mismatched. Your marriage was contracted for convenience sake; you were incompatible and unsuitable for each other from the beginning. You, fly, tried to make a bee out of a bumblebee at the risk that, were this possible you would have become the queen of the beehive and never ceased to be pregnant. You ignored the fact that the nature of the bumblebee was to fleet from flower to flower, to pollinate them and not to bring any honey back home. Had you known that bumblebees were not good material for a husband, you would never have married him. And you, husband, you too cannot turn a fly into a bee.

Neither of you have to stay in abusive relationship. You can divorce with impunity and I, Dr. Free Foodstaples, will see to it that neither of you starve. You do not need to wait for an act of god, or for the staging of bloody uprising! Has not French and Russian Revolution taught you anything?

Our present social situation is like a bad marriage. It was initially contracted as a marriage of convenience. A divorce of the business, whose function it is to create goods and services, from the imposed obligation to care for the workers' personal needs is therefore 'devoutly to be wish'd,' as neither business could be run like a family nor a family run like a business.

We created our social system, so we humans have to get rid of it and build a better one. All it takes is enough of us to want to do it, and the will to fight for it. It means that it was 'we' in collusion with 'them,' not 'they' alone who created this system. And it is we and not they alone, who at the present time keep this system alive and well, and who resist attempts to dis-empower it.

ON THE SUBJECT OF DIGNITY

What is human dignity? How does one achieve it? What sort of human dignity vaccinates one against depression, drug and alcohol abuse? Does job training and holding a job promotes real social change? Does it confer dignity? Does education pertain to teaching what human dignity is really about, or how to fit into the mold of a life of indignities and learn to like it?

Five hundred years ago, Italian scholar by the name of Pico dela Mirandola wrote a treatise titled "Oration on the Dignity of Man." In it he said these words, as he imagined God giving instructions to Adam after his creation: "Neither a fixed abode nor a form that is thine alone nor any function peculiar to thyself have we given thee, Adam, to the end that according to thy longing and according to thy judgment thou mayest have and possess what abode, what form, and what functions thou thyself shalt desire.... Thou, constrained by no limits, in accordance with thine own free will, in whose hands We have placed thee, shalt ordain for thyself the limits of thy nature...We have made thee neither of heaven nor of earth, neither mortal nor immortal, so that with freedom of choice and with honour, as though the maker and molder of thyself, though mayest fashion thyself in whatever shape thou shalt prefer. Thou shalt have the power to degenerate into the lower forms of life, which are brutish. Thou shalt have the power, out of thy soul's judgment, to be reborn into the higher forms, which are divine. Beasts as soon as they were born brought with them from their mother's womb all they would ever possess, but thou are not a beast."

What is the essence of the indignity of being a slave? It is having no choice but to work if one did not want to die. In other words to be a slave is like being a beast of burden. In essence, this formula has not changed since the Pharaoh's times. Perhaps we made a slight progress in that the threats of death by starvation nowadays are somewhat veiled: "You don't have to work if you don't want to, but...!"

In philosophical sense one could say that slavery and tyranny never existed, because if one disregarded unpleasant and deadly consequence of one's actions, one has always been free to resist, to oppose and to question. Nowadays of course there is a Code of Human Rights. One can choose for whom to slave and the employer is severely limited in his treatment of those who work (slave) for him. With the increasing rate of unemployment many people wish they could slave for someone but there are no takers, no slave masters. Thus the essence of slavery is obfuscated.

A social milieu in which human dignity could be achieved does not exist at present in our society, nor in any society in the world, since one is deprived of the freedom to choose in accordance with the ideological mandate that: 'everyone is free to choose to be anything, provided he chooses to be a worker.' Thus his preoccupation with his own survival and with that of his immediate family, saps all his time and strength, and deprives him of the opportunity to fashion himself into the shape of his choice of preference. This mandate lowers him to the level of a beast, which in the eyes of the above named Italian scholar has no dignity.

Being born with a silver spoon in one's mouth, and not worrying where the next meal will come from, constitutes an ideal social and economic setup, in which human dignity could be achieved. However, there are not enough silver spoons to go around and those who become wealthy only by the sweat of their brow are not equally fated. This is so because by the time they get into position to be free to mold themselves into the shape they 'freely and honorably choose,' they are firmly set in the mold of money-makers, money-changers, or just conspicuous consumers of manufactured goods.

BORN FREE

A child is born free. He is provided with all the amenities important for his growth and development. Within the bounds set up for him by his family structure, he has the opportunity to be socialized, and to choose his mode of being. It is mandated that he be educated. The Law protects him from being drafted into the army and exploited on the labour market. This setup facilitates his growth. He has to be given food and shelter free of charge. He is in his prime to enjoy a dignified existence.

However, while the child grows up he is constantly harangued that he must have an identity, i.e. that he must know who he is, that he must find himself, provided that he finds himself to be a worker. In other words he must make plans on what he wants to become: the butcher, the baker, or the candlestick maker. He has no choice to be nobody in particular; he has to become somebody.

His human dignity is crushed the minute he reaches an independent existence as an adult. If until then he did not succeed in becoming what he wanted to be, or if what he had chosen to become lost its market value, he is delegated to lead an existence of a stray domestic animal foraging for food. Now, foraging for food in a society has to be done in a socially acceptable manner, not by hunting, fishing, or harvesting fruits of nature, but by selling (trading) oneself or one's services for money to put food on the table. In other words he has to earn living. He is not free not to trade. He is forced to work, i.e. he is forced to trade.

What he has to offer must be marketable. This means that the dignity of molding himself into his preferred shape, in the words of Pico dela Mirandola, "with freedom of choice and with honour, as though the maker and molder of himself" would have to be abandoned if a buyer could not be found. With great indignity he would then be forced to forgo his dignity of being a human and degenerate into the brutish forms of life in order to keep body and soul together.

He may be subjected to further indignity of 'job training program,' meaning that he, the human being, maker and molder of himself, was given no other choice but be trained to become a robot. For the next 30 years he would have to renounce all that is human in him and keep slugging it out as a robot. Occasionally, to lift his spirits he would take a drink or antidepressant medication. Finally, at the age of 50 years, as an obsolete and unprofitable baggage, he would be terminated and replaced by more sophisticated robots. With his brain shriveled up from chronic disuse, he would lie there on the heap of retirees, holding a dented can of tuna in his hand, contemplating the indignity of his human situation.

As our young person matures and becomes married, he is beset by number of children, as the result of which the dignity of molding himself becomes fossilized at a faster rate, as his total existence is drained of time and energy to become something else than a breadwinner. He might have to come to terms with, what he considered to be the indignity of being a bus driver, a welder, a security guard, a janitor, or whatever have you. Such an act would be construed by his contemporaries as paying back to the society his dues.

In order not to be misunderstood let me stress that I do not think that there are any shameful or undignified occupations in life. The indignity consists only in being forced into a mode of being which, were it not for the threat to him or to his family's welfare, he would never choose, and out of which there is no escape. Being blackmailed into activity by socially engineered environment, starvation, or other threats to one's welfare, is despicable and criminal. However, as a freely chosen act, undertaken for whatever purpose, other than food, it is one of dignified means to an end, which one has an inborn right to pursue. Not everyone will agree with this definition, as what is dignified in one context may be shameful, sinful, or illegal in another one. According to the Islamic Law for example, in some African countries it is shameful for some Arabs to do physical work, even if freely chosen.

It is a waste of human resources to harness everyone into the process of foraging for food and seeking shelter. Many talents remain untapped simply because a person is involved in the process of putting food on the table. It is true that one gets paid much more than just for food, constituting sufficient amounts of money to enable him to eat for weeks and months. But this fact alone does not free him from continuous and uninterrupted presence at the workbench or in the office. No matter how much money he earns, the time to use it to enable him "to be reborn into higher forms of being, which are divine," is sadly lacking. Thus although he could achieve greatness, he is forced to acquiesce to the existence as a worker and a consumer of goods.

The problem is that jobs come in packages of 40 hours a week plus overtime, and there are not enough jobs to employ everyone. It's possible that working 5 hours a week could earn enough for subsistence. A certificate of having fulfilled such a requirement would be sufficient to receive one week's supply of food staples. The availability of jobs from one, two, three, ...20... 40... or more hours per week, at all times, would give the person an opportunity to work as much as he desired and perhaps fade out gradually from the workforce rather than ever completely retire. (Workfare requires a person to put 19 hours a month of community work to qualify to receive sustenance for one month). The continuous and uninterrupted availability of hourly jobs to guarantee the freedom from hunger is however an utopian dream.

FREEDOM NOT TO WORK

Understanding the 'expectation of consequences' helps us to determine how 'free' we are to do something. Because the consequences of our choices depend on our circumstances, and all of us find ourselves in different circumstances, some of which are so dire that the freedom to choose practically does not exist. Beggars for instance are not choosers.

A person held up at a gunpoint, theoretically has a choice to part with his money or his life. However his choice is not free. The same person sitting behind the bullet-proof glass, or being surrounded by security guards, or having knowledge that the gun pointed at him is either a toy-gun or not loaded, has considerably more options available to him. He is freer, because he is in more favourable circumstances.

Analogous to the hold-up situation, a hungry person with a hungry family to feed, without a penny in his pocket and without a job, finds himself in a dire situation in which the number of options available to him is so small that it is tantamount to having no choice. He has to either give up his and his family's life, or give up his human dignity and 'choose' what is wrong, distasteful, or backbreaking, in order to live.

One can ask here a rhetorical question: What psychological need dos it serve to place food out of reach of others and then ask them to work hard to get it and in the course of getting it give them an excess of money, which they do not need, and then coax them to spend it on life's amenities which they do not desire? Should not these people have the right to receive their daily bread without doing any work?

Some more questions: What psychological needs of a giver does it fill to give the hungry a meaningless sum of money of undetermined value, insufficient to keep him housed and fed, and call it a social safety net? Would not a person be better served if he was given no money with its illusory feeling of security, but given instead a constitutionally guaranteed assurance that 'no one in this society will starve, freeze to death, die of a medically curable disease, be unable to move from place to place or be uneducated.' Would such a person not be better served if governments stayed out business of distributing wealth, worrying how to occupy his idle hands and how to make everyone wealthy, happy, healthy, knowledgeable, skillful, important, responsible and useful?

When food is grown in abundance in this country, what perverted needs does it serve to terrorize the population with the notion that there will not be enough money in the till to feed everybody, that a pension plan will be broke by the time the baby-boomers retire, etc.? Why does one support the system which hires highly paid welfare and social workers to humiliate the supplicants begging food, and asks them to go on fruitless errand of job hunting, requiring them to show thirty different places of employment they visited each month? Why is one willing to part with his hard earned dollar in order that the government offers it as a subsidy to a prospective job creator? And finally, why to work if there is nothing to do? Why to produce if there is no need for the product? One hardly ever hears a complaint the we need more clothes or more cars or more TV sets, but the refrain "Jobs, jobs, jobs" constantly rings in our ears.

It is true that we have a limited choice of jobs, but ironically, just having such a choice limits our freedom. One just can imagine how would one feel if someone made him an 'offer which he could not refuse' and said to him: "Either this or that, it's your choice," or "You have only three choices!" "The choice is yours." If one is *forced* to choose then the choice is a forced one. The command: "Your money or your life!" gives one a choice but does not make him free to choose. Why not? Because he is not free to refuse to make such a choice. Philosophically speaking, our freedom has never been lost, nor ever can be lost. It is only the dread of consequences that "puzzles the will and makes us rather bear those ills we know, than fly to others that we know not of" (Hamlet's soliloquy).

The lack of *freedom not to work* is the last bastion to be overcome on the way to a totally free and just society. Thus, it is not work but the socially mandated *compulsion* to work that should be entirely eliminated. Without this basic freedom there can be no human dignity. Freedom to work, or not to work, is equivalent to the freedom to trade, or not to trade. Working, after all, is trading of something we can perform for money. Free trade agreement between the counties guarantees governments' non-interference with free flow of goods. However the free trade does not force any given country to trade. There are many trade embargoes in the world to testify to this fact.

On individual level we are free to refuse to sell our property unless it is for the good of community, in which case we can be expropriated against our will. For the good of society we also can be prohibited from selling tobacco, liquor, or guns to a minor. However when it comes to survival we are mandated to have money to trade for food, which translates into compulsory trading of our job performance for money.

All freedoms, to qualify as freedoms, have to contain in themselves their opposites. Freedom of movement allows a person to move about without restriction, but does not mandate that he be on the move. Freedom of speech allows person to express an opinion but does not force him to speak out his mind. Freedom of religion permits one to worship any or no deity, but does not mandate that one must be a believer. Freedom of assembly and of association permits one to socialize with anyone but does not dictate that one must not be a recluse. Freedom to work does not qualify as freedom because it does not include in itself its opposite, i.e. freedom not to work. It is an oxymoron. It is like saying that a slave is free not to slave, or a man who *has* to work is at the same time free not to work.

A horse is born a horse and is doomed to be nothing but a horse until his death. He has no choice but to repay to the society the debt for his fodder of oats. He is fed and work is forcefully extracted from him. There is no dignity in it. Saddling him with a ruby-studded saddle would not add even one iota to his dignity.

Presently our human dignity is supposed to come from being designated as a worker, and then from a paycheck and a job description: the more money and the less dirt, the greater dignity. We could then sweeten the indignity of our human situation by spending our income on entertainment, which would lift our spirits. A slave, however, does not become hoodwinked into thinking that he is free by just having his spirit lifted by spending the money earned. Setting him free, by guaranteeing his inalienable right to be free from hunger and cold would permit his own creative genius to do the lifting up of his spirits for him.

Dignity is not related to the rate of pay or to the kind of labour one performs. Cleaning the septic tanks for *no* wages is more dignified if one does it out of one's free will. Dignity resides in freedom. To be forced to work is undignified at any price. Although there is no dignity in being confined to be just a worker, there is even less dignity in being displaced from the workplace and becoming reliant on meager welfare, or to be given even more menial labour at lower rate of pay.

In the final analysis, freedom not to work is neither revolutionary idea nor something with which we are unfamiliar. The idea is shocking because it is expressed in stark naked terms, without any qualifying subordinate clauses. As such it is unrecognizable. Freedom not having to work for food staples sounds milder and more reassuring. It is equivalent with the phrase 'labour-saving devices.' We ought to be free not to work by washing dishes by hand, by digging ditches with pickaxe and shovel, by walking to the office on foot, by traveling to another city by horse and buggy. And we already enjoy such freedom now. We call them labour-saving devices. They set us free with respect to the specific jobs mentioned above. No one is ashamed to use such devices. No one fears the risk of being called lazy and running away from hard work by using the electrical appliances as one's slaves. In a similar fashion, we should develop labour-saving set-up, which would free us from having to work for food staples. The free food staples plan constitutes such a labour-saving instrument. Of course it has to be paid for, like everything else. There is no need to repeat: 'there are no free lunches!"

DEFINITION OF WORK

The word 'work' has many connotations. Broadly defined, work means 'putting out effort to accomplish an end.' In this sense everything in nature works because everything is in a constant state of flux. Life is a continuity of movement from moment to moment, and movement is work. Nothing ever is dead because nothing is ever at a standstill.

Work in political and economic sense is "an effort put out to accomplish a goal *for money.*" In practical terms, since it is impossible to live without moving, without putting out effort, which requires expenditure of energy, working and getting paid are synonymous. Thus, to work and *not get paid* for it equates with 'doing nothing,' whereas doing nothing and *getting paid* for it equates with 'working.'

Our attitude towards work is ambivalent; work is a reward, when it is freely chosen (think of hobbies), and work is a punishment if it is imposed on one by others. Since everyone *has to* work in order to eat, work has most of the time a punitive connotation, i.e. everyone has to *suffer* in a biblical sense in order to eat. This unpleasant aspect of work breeds resentment amongst the taxpayers: "Why should he, the taxpayer, suffer working and pay high taxes to support a leisurely life style of a sloth?" Hence the idea of workfare: 'Let them eat their bread in the sweat of their brow.'

We also show great ambivalence towards the idea of beneficial effect of working per se. It is good for us but we don't know why. And not knowing why, we acquiesce to the idea that those who know why, should be in position of authority to force us to work for our own good. The implication of this question is that normally nothing in nature works unless force is applied. Based on this assumption it follows that no person would work if he did not have to, the main motivating factor being to put food on the table. This might perhaps be the main reason why removing this incentive (to make living) is fraught with fear that the world would, so to say, go into a catatonic stupor when this happened. However, even a superficial observation of the reality confirms the opposite: it is impossible to force a person to be idle.

The word 'work' translated into Russian means 'robota,' and in Czech 'robota' means 'compulsory labour.' The word 'worker' in Russian means 'robotnik.' In other words, work is a robotic process. It is compulsory because a mechanical, electronic or human robot cannot of itself change a given programming. Secondly, the process is suitable for programming and therefore repetitive and lacking in flexibility. Thus to be called a worker is not exactly a dignifying or flattering designation.

My definition of work is more convoluted: Work is the suffering inflicted on me by an agent or agency other than myself, by *making me* perform a function which this agency considers to be "good." By the word "making me" I mean using all sorts of coercion, threats (overt or implied), and arbitrarily placing in the path of my pursuit of happiness socially engineered obstacles, in such a way as to make me bypass them and, in this act of bypassing, forcing me to do what I would not do if such obstacles were not there.

Eating itself is a hard work. This becomes apparent when we separate the process of eating into various activities which make eating possible, e.g.: fishing and hunting, slaughtering, harvesting, shopping, delivering food to one's house, chopping, cooking, serving meals and dish-washing. Each of these activities qualifies as full time remunerative employment. This is what cavemen, hunters, and pioneer farmers used to do centuries ago. This is what every creature in nature does. To track an antelope and to eat it, a lion has to work.

It is a reflection on how deeply we have been indoctrinated with work ethic, that we consider the freedom not to work synonymous with freedom to do nothing. I personally have gone through periods of being unemployed, but although I did not work I did more things than during my working hours.

In every day's experience, to work means to do as one was told: start work at certain hour, be properly attired, smile at the customers, push paper, walk floors, tighten the bolts on the assembly line, peddle specified products, do not idle, do not conduct your private business during working hours, do not make mistakes, do not daydream, etc., etc., and get paid at the end of the day.

In reality then, to work means *to do nothing else than* what the work requires one to do. It means that for a specified period of time one agrees to be designated as a robot. In practical terms, at the end of the working day one is so exhausted that one is ready for a bottle of beer and a nap, and *nothing* else. On the other hand *not having to work* means 'freedom to do everything,' which naturally also includes doing nothing. In summary, to have to work for one's subsistence deprives one of human dignity by forcing one to do nothing.

THE WORK ETHIC

The work ethic means: " If you do not want to starve to death, you have to work for money to buy yourself something to eat." Premier of Ontario, Mike Harris's Workfare is the prime example of the work ethic in its stark naked form. It tells the recipient of the welfare that he must perform some type of work imposed on him by the creators of workfare in order to deserve to be fed and stay alive. The Work Ethic then is the general form of Workfare. It tells everyone, without exception, that the only reason why they are permitted to eat and stay alive is because they, or someone else on their behalf, worked on a job created for him by the economic machine, to make it possible. The disabled are excepted from this rule. This is hypocritical because no one in any society is sentenced to death by starvation if he is healthy but refuses to work. So why do we play 'hard to get' by saying 'no' to the lazy if we know that we will say 'yes' to him in the end?

The work ethic demands that each newborn justify, in an animal fashion, his appearance on the world's stage. Like an animal he has to make himself useful to other people if he wants to be fed. Were he in reality an animal and unproductive he would be fattened up and slaughtered for food.

Those who maintain that we are already working voluntarily under the present system of food distribution, must be doing it philosophically, meaning that no one can be forced to do anything against his will, ergo people *choose* to work *in order not to starve*. Of course they choose to, but so does a person who gives his money away to the robber "voluntarily," when a gun is pointed at his head, *in order not to get shot*.

Work ethic and being *forced to work for food* are inseparable. We made great strides in desisting from resorting to violence when people refused to do what they were supposed to do. Not so long ago it was a criminal offence to refuse to live, and anyone attempting suicide had to appear before the judge. Now we can refuse to recite Lord's Prayer, to go to church, to shut up, to lead a healthy style of life, to be treated for life-threatening illnesses, to stay in marriage or to have a particular job. One thing we still cannot refuse to do is *to work*. The obverse of this is, that *if* we cannot refuse, then we have to.

To artificially interpolate work between a person and his need to eat is unconscionable. Were I the creator, I would consider putting artificial obstacles between my creatures, and the food necessary for their survival, as a violation of my will, tantamount to killing, and as such an unpardonable sin!

This work ethic by itself is the main cause of bloody revolutions, which never accomplished anything revolutionary in the past. The suggested instantaneous social rebirth in this book does not consist in bloodletting, or killing the goose that lays the golden egg. The quiet revolution consists of the insight and recognition that eating is biologically determined and not a subject to the vagaries of the stock market, GNP, or the unemployment rate. Free food staples for everyone is a revolutionary idea for 21st century. It kills one hundred birds with one stroke and puts an end to all social systems now in existence.

The following *PARABLE OF RAINING LOONIES* poignantly caricatures the above process of interpolating work and money between person's need to eat and the food necessary for his survival.

From the war-torn Burgonia a cry for help was heard. People were on the verge of starvation. The taxpayers of the world responded to their plea and agreed to construct several gigantic food-warehouses, to be guarded by their military might. However, a dispute arose as to how to distribute this freely donated food and who of the people would be considered worthy of receiving it. Agreement was finally reached that it would have to be paid for with Canadian dollars, but since no Burgonians possessed any of the Canadian currency, it would have to be given to them as a part of an aid. A decision to do it that way was based on the need to educate Burgonians that there are no free lunches and that every scrap of food they consumed would have to be paid for. However, the problem still remained of how to distribute the currency? An ingenious process of delivery was invented: Loonies (Canadian $1 coins) would rain on Burgonia from the sky, one loony per person per day multiplied by the estimated size of the population.

The rationale for this solution was simple: Since loonies did not really come from heaven and somebody had to work to produce them, Burgonians also had to put out effort to get them. It was in harmony with biblical injunction that man should eat his bread in the sweat of his brow until he returned to the ground. More jobs would be created in Canada to mint loonies and as a byproduct it would help Canadian economy. Also exercise could contribute to Burgonians' good physical health.

Giant cargo planes braved anti-aircraft fire and commenced a steady drizzle of loonies over Burgonia. At sunrise, Burgonians rushed out of their houses and, like children hunting for Easter Eggs at Easter, began scouring the landscape. Some stepped on mines and lost their legs or their lives. Taxpayers of the world were firm in their resolution. That was life --they said--their pilots also risked losing their lives; Burgonians had to be taught to take responsibility for themselves.

More aggressive ones procured loony-detectors, and soon the manufacture of those detectors made the entrepreneurs very rich. Others began to form corporations and with heavy machinery methodically sieved through every inch of the Burgonian soil. Workers had to be hired and paid 10 cents for each loony found. Rumors had it that some Burgonians were being chauffeured in Mercedes Benz limousines and some even opened bank accounts in Switzerland.

It came to pass that there arouse a shortage of loonies because of the protracted strike of the miners who mined nickel, zinc and copper ores for loonies. In addition several cargo-planes were shot down and the price of their replacement skyrocketed. Minimum wages of the mint workers and the price of food went up. A painful dilemma faced the taxpayers of the world: Either the taxes would have to be increased or the rain of loonies drastically reduced or even discontinued. The last alternative was untenable, as it would have ushered in a food shortage of famine like proportions.

One of the world taxpayers came up with an ingenious solution: "Why do we need loonies and the loony-cargo-planes at all —he said. Could we not feed Burgonians directly with food? Then we would not need to increase our taxes." Everyone agreed and thus *humanitarian aid,* as we know it, was born and taxes were kept at the same level.

The road to sanity lies in putting away the principle that everyone must have money to pay for his daily bread each time he sat down for a meal, and do what is right, by substituting for it the principle that 'collectively we must have enough money to put into the pot, to prepay for food which we will be consuming in the future.' This would enable lunches to be free on a prepaid basis.

GENESIS OF WORK ETHIC

Work ethic is an ideology. It is a culturally doctored frame of mind rather than a result of natural necessity or scientific argumentation. It is a programming of our minds that leaves no room for deviation. Going against it brings onto the deviant 'the wrath of gods' in the form of guilt that one has done something wrong, requiring a corrective action to stay the course.

It behooves us to know how did we come to acquire this belief, called work ethic, for if we do not know how we got it, we will not know how to get rid of it. The admonition that 'he who does not work shall not eat' comes from the Bible. It comes from the teaching of religious doctrine of having to work as a punishment for the commission of the original sin. Later it was accepted by governments as a modicum of feeding people at the time of food scarcity and finally as the natural way of food distribution in times of plenty.

The paraphrased version from Genesis reads: "And to Adam, God said: Because you listened to your wife and ate the fruit when I told you not to, I have placed a *curse upon the soil*. All your life you will struggle to extract a living from it. It will grow thorns and thistles for you, and you shall eat its grasses. All your life you will sweat to master it, until your dying days."

The second passage which constitutes the backbone of the work ethic is the verbatim quotation from the letter which St. Paul wrote to the church of Thessalonica: "For you well know that you ought to follow our example: you never saw us *loafing;* we never accepted food from anyone *without buying it;* we *worked hard day and night for the money we needed to live on,* in order that we would not be a burden to any of you. It wasn't that we didn't have the right to ask you to feed us, but we wanted to show you, firsthand, *how you should work for your living.* Even while we were still there with you we gave you this rule: '*He who does not work shall not eat.* '"

The passages quoted from the Bible are full of truisms. One does not have to be a Bible scholar, nor have an access to divine wisdom, to know that one cannot eat what one does not have, and that to have food one has to put out effort to get it. There is no great philosophy in it. It is ideological only in the sense, that if we accept that there was a Creator of this world, there must also have been reason why he created it. One of those reasons is supposed to be the entrapment of Adam into disobedience and then punishing him and his descendants for the sin he committed when he ate the forbidden fruit.

The passages mean what they say: *a curse* was placed upon the soil and to extract living from it required struggle accompanied by the sweat of one's face. This is a statement of fact. No one disagrees with it. Eating for the most part consists of obtaining food, i.e. tilling the cursed land, sowing, reaping, fishing, hunting, and trudging to the supermarket. Of course the biblical writers could not have used such words as: "supermarket," or "prepaid", because in their times no one would have understood what they were talking bout. And they were obviously not referring to the sweating for Imperial Oil or General Motors.

The entire animal kingdom partakes of the same wisdom. When a lion gets hungry he knows that he has to get himself some food. So, he goes on a hunt. He lies in wait for a zebra to come by, and makes a kill. Then he drags the carcass to a safe place to dismember it. It isn't easy. We ourselves could not do it without the help of cutting tools. We can only imagine what the reaction of this lion would be, if prior to going on a hunt, the work-ethic-ideologue asked him to deliver a heavy load some distance away to earn the privilege.

From this observation we can deduct that the creative act, if such ever there was, consisted of two inseparable aspects: a lion and the food necessary for his sustenance placed within his easy reach. If there were no food pools for the lion to dip into, "in a socialist-like fashion," regardless of his input, then there would be no lions on earth, and we would not even know that lions ever existed.

Of course, when the Bible was written, whoever did not go fishing or did not pluck the fruit from a tree, he could not eat. The same law applies now as then: whoever does not fetch food from the grocery store, and carry it home, then prepare it, cook it, and chew it, he also cannot eat what he does not have. If he does not eat then he dies. In this case god does not withhold food, but the person intent on not eating is either sick, or starves himself to death in a suicidal attempt. Eating is hard work and no one refusing to perform such work of eating, should be spoon-fed or tube-fed by force. Not much has changed.

The simple refutation of the idea that god himself might be withholding food from the sloths is the fact that he placed food within the human reach and *not* somewhere high up on a mountain, while asking all his creatures to tread on steps of a treadmill (probably manufacturing some plastic gargoyles), on the way to it

I grew up on a farm and when the lunchtime came, mother sent me to get a few potatoes from the garden. It took me a few minutes to stick a fork into the ground, pull out the plant and end up with some five potatoes, enough for one meal for the entire family. That was my sweat for the day. When recently my wife asked me to get potatoes from the supermarket, it turned out to be a hard labour. Without a car, I had to walk some twelve blocks to the nearest supermarket, get a bag of potatoes weighing 10 lbs and carry it back home. In the sweat of my face did I eat my supper that day.

THE SCARS OF
WORK ETHIC CONDITIONING

It is pitiful to observe what havoc centuries of indoctrination with the work ethic has wrought on human dignity, when a man who was born a creator vies with animals, machines, computers and virtual workers for a place at the workbench! Why in the world would a human being yearn to perform monotonous, repetitive, stultifying and sometimes backbreaking jobs, which the lower forms of life are so well adopted to perform? How low can a human being sink when a person feels guilty about loafing, is at a loss to know what to do with himself, and like an ox awaits a driver to put a yoke on him, crack the whip and create for him a purpose of his life!

Some people justify the reign of work ethic on grounds that: "Even in a pure socialist states, one still had to work." The use of the word "even" is surprising, because it is *only* under the socialist and communist dictatorships that one had to work. There were no free lunches without work. Possession of money alone in order to subsist, without having worked for it, smacked of criminal activity and was on equal footing with theft, embezzlement, counterfeiting, etc. It was also on equal footing with such capitalistic business practices as renting out property, charging interests on loans, and exploiting the labour of other people for one's gains. Under the Napoleonic law one was guilty until proven innocent, meaning that one could be hauled before the judge to explain how it was possible to subsist without working. Forced labour and re-education in concentration camps followed as a punishment

In the western democracies just "showing the money" is enough to enable one to have a 'free' lunch, i.e. without the need to prove that one had worked for it. It is presumed that all money in circulation is legitimately obtained, and whosoever questions it would be well advised to keep his thoughts to himself, or lay charges by supplying the supporting evidence and risk the counter suit for libel.

Talking about work in the Western democracies smacks of socialism. Glorification of work is an ideology. It was practiced to the hilt in the former Soviet Union as it is now in Cuba. There the medal was given out as a reward for the outstanding production on assembly line, and only the workers were chosen to enter the workers' paradise. Workers were valuable horses that enjoyed all the privileges due to horses. Fat and lazy bourgeois were dispensable pigs, confined to a pigsty. During the Chinese Cultural Revolution, every 'non-working' intellectual was obliged to get a whiff of real work on the farm. In those countries it was criminal to leave home without going to work.

It is therefore surprising that such *socialist* practices, as organizing welfare recipients into a workforce to perform workfare, harvesting food on a farm just for food, threatening refusniks with starvation if they refused to work for their sustenance, were allowed to creep undetected, under the guise of *workfare*, into the bastions of capitalism, as it exists in U.S. and Canada.

MECHANISM OF COMPULSION
– SOCIAL ENGINEERING

It is said that money is the source of all evil. However, capital has no inherent power over us. It is merely an entry in the bankbook, a pile of paper or metal, a collection of coins and banknotes, tokens in a Monopoly game, a gun empty of bullets. It represents certain value, which could be exchanged for other values, a pile of something, a collection of cars, horses, castles, art objects, etc. It is an ideal means of exchange replacing the cumbersome barter system.

So what is the mechanism of this compulsion, if it is not the need to subsist? What else in the world, one may ask, *compels* one to work for the profit of someone else? There are two meanings to the word 'compulsion': It either comes from within oneself in the shape of *strong desire* to do something, or it comes from outside and is tantamount to *blackmail*.

It is difficult for some people to realize that we live in a socially engineered environment in which we are manipulated by the policy we adopt in such a way as to be forced (i.e. to have no other choice but) to freely choose that which the society wants us to. We are free to choose everything, which is not expressly forbidden, provided that we choose what the government wants us to choose.

A good example of social engineering is the one that was practiced in the former Soviet Union with regards to the collectivization program. The small farmers refused to give up their privately owned farms and join the large, state owned collectives. They were told that, of course they were free under the Soviet Constitution to join the collectives or to continue on their own. However, it was pointed out to them that the drain on their income would make it unprofitable for them to do so, since the government would demand from them increasingly higher and higher taxes until they were unable to pay them, at what point it would take over their farm as a payment for taxes in arrears.

To exemplify social engineering in action I will quote from "The Parable of Homo-electric Power:"

When, in the principality of Conundrum, the riverbeds dried up and the waterfalls were reduced to a trickle, electric power had to be generated using human muscles. A giant wheel, mounted horizontally onto the gearbox of the electric generator, was kept in motion by 12 men abreast behind each of the 8 spokes of the wheel. A number of such generators sprung up throughout the principality providing it with ample amount of electric power and at the same time solving the problem of unemployment and preserving the ideology of the work ethic.

High wages and labour strikes made homo-electric power uneconomical and the government asked the Courts to declare the generation of the electric power as an essential service, and mandate the workers to return back to work, passing the law making strikes illegal. There followed an increased incidence of accidents, absenteeism from work, violent clashes, legal prosecutions and incarcerations making the enforcement of this law prohibitively expensive and producing increased number of power outages.

Mr. Foxworthy, a practicing social engineer, was consulted. He was given a task to engineer the production of electricity without large outlay of money, without resorting to violence and without enforcing the law and prosecuting the law-breakers. Workers should be given *full freedom to work or not to work* in the generator plants -- he was told-- produce electricity without getting paid, and praise the Lord for being given the opportunity to do so.

Mr. Foxworthy considered an option of pumping water to higher elevations and searched for the way of making people carry pails of water uphill. Once the reservoir was filled – he thought -- all one would have to do is to open the sluice gate and activate the generators. As he procrastinated he was suddenly gripped by Eureka experience.

He said to himself: Although you cannot make anyone carry water up the hill, human nature makes people carry their own weight. An average person, weighing 80 Kg., carried on him an equivalent of 80 liters of water (ca. 20 gallons) If he could be motivated to go uphill and then ride down on the paddle wheel of a generator, over and over again, he would replace water as a source of energy and himself become a renewable, dry source of energy, without posing the usual dangers to the environment through flooding. Most important of all was the *preservation of the freedom not to work.*

He also had an answer to those critics who maintained that no one in his right mind could be convinced to participate in this project to make it work. His opinion was that, if the law mandated all grocery stores to be located on the twenty-fifth floor of a building, everyone in need of groceries would have to make the climb. And then, in order to get down they would have a choice either to walk downstairs, or to take down the gravity operated elevator. The elevator incidentally operated the electric generator. He was certain that everyone would avail himself of this convenience, especially when carrying a heavy load of groceries.

There was also a sound rationale to locate all grocery stores on the twenty-fifth floor, which came to him as an afterthought, in that the real estate was at a premium and in the absence of ample truck-loading zones, it made a good sense to deliver food to the store by a helicopter, which could conveniently land on the roof.

As Mr. Foxworthy contemplated additional rationale of locating grocery stores on the twenty-fifth floor his eyes fell, as if by divine guidance, on the newspaper article in which a team of scientists found a correlation between carcinogens in food, loss of nutritive food value, and the distance from the ground at which food was stored. There was higher incidence of cancer amongst those who ate food stored at the ground level.

The researchers found that every three meters (or the average height of one floor of a building) the carcinogens diminished by a small percentage and the life of the product increased. The jury was still out on whether this was due to electromagnetic forces, traces of radon gases, sulfuric content of flatulence, concentration of pollutants close to the ground, or some yet unknown mysterious substance "X".

Whatever the findings, the ministry of health of the principality jumped quickly on the wagon. In all conscience –it said-- it could not afford to take the risk of exposing its people to the ground-level-food. It sent out a warning that eating food stored at the ground level for appreciable time was hazardous to one's health and done at the consumers own risk. Location of grocery stores on the twenty-fifth floor thus became the law.

Not everyone, however, had to walk up twenty-five floors to get groceries, which incidentally was free of charge. One was able to purchase a "smart card" which permitted one to take an elevator up. The disabled got their card as a part of their social assistance. Only the poor and able-bodied ones had to climb and thus paid their debt to the society. Of course, the smart card was also available to them for a price, provided that they were involved in some other remunerative employment. Thus, the unpleasant connotation of workfare was avoided.

It came to pass that budgetary deficit was on the increase and economic depression set in. The cost of living went up. To counteract it, the location of the supermarkets had to be raised by another ten floors and the price of the smart cards increased. In times of crisis a temporary ten-stories high tower was added to the level of the supermarket and people were encouraged, for a price of a ticket, to climb to observe through the telescope the volcanic eruptions on the Jupiter's moon Io. When the terrain was unsuitable for thirty-five story building, a series of revolving doors were installed before the entrance to the store. They served the same purpose as gravity operated elevators.

Thus, Mr. Foxworthy solved the economic problems of the Principality of Conundrum. The homo-electric power was generated, the surplus of which was sold abroad and earned for the principality some profits. No one cared whether anyone worked or not. Most importantly, there were no slaves and everyone lived happily ever after.

THE RATIONALE FOR
FREE FOOD STAPLES PLAN

It is a self-evident fact that:

1. human dependence on food is mandated by its biology and cannot be altered by any other considerations;
2. every person alive at this moment has been eating;
3. the average nutritional requirement for survival has been the same for each individual from the time of his first beginning, throughout the entire world, given a narrow range of statistical deviation;
4. hunger, starvation, and famines are a social fact and not a natural one, the result of human arrangement and not an act of god.

Everything necessary or desirable for human life is in abundance, but we create scarcity and then try to carefully manage and allocate the use of our resources. In Christian mythology God created the devil and, in his mysterious ways, has been giving him sustenance ever since. We are not any different: we create evil and say: there is evil. We create scarcity of resources and say: there is a scarcity. We close our eyes and say: we cannot see.

All political systems in the world are governed by businesses competing for profits. This is our highest ideal. Everything is good if it is profitable. Thus, we create evil because fighting evil is profitable. We create poverty because fighting poverty is a big business. We do not legalize drugs because fighting the drug trafficking is profitable. We create hostilities between the countries and fight wars because armament and wars is profitable. Even now we are probably on the look out for an Evil Empire, because peace may not pay as high dividends. The Free Food Staples Plan (subscribed to, or prepaid for) is probably less profitable; therefore businesses competing for profits may have none of it.

Such an economic system is not sustainable because, with better education and the spread of information on the Internet, people will soon start rebelling against increased exploitation and the depletion of natural resources. The environment will fight back against further pollution and destruction by staging increased number of natural cataclysms. The avalanche of unconsumed surpluses, plus garbage will bury us alive. In addition, our financial crises consisting of mounting national debt and yearly budgetary deficits will grow worse. With increasing numbers of unemployed and poor, there will not be enough money to go around. Printing more money will only fuel inflation. Feeding people via job creation will become impossible with only 20% of people working. There is no other way!

Subsistence must come first and this ought to be freely accessible to everyone, unconditional of his work status. No one should be starved into employment. Only he should work who wanted to, motivated by the availability of the consumer goods and the desire to acquire them. If there were no consumer goods on the shelves, what would one do with the money earned? And if the answer is: 'nothing' then why would one want to work at all? The Soviet Union went bankrupt because rubles could not buy much, and no one was anxious to do his best to acquire large amount of rubles.

WHAT FREE FOOD STAPLES PLAN IS NOT

The free food staples plan is not some version of Food Stamps program as it is practiced in the U.S. Food Stamps are the wrong solution to the hunger problem. These are the reasons:

1) Stamps could be exchanged for money, in which case families would not get the basic food requirements. 2) The program is not universal but discriminatory: only the poor people get it. 3) It perpetuates and juxtaposes the two social classes: the poor, who need the social assistance in order to subsist, and the rich, whose largesse makes the subsistence of the poor possible. 4) The haves, who pay for Food Stamps, resent footing the bill without themselves being the beneficiaries thereof. This resentment threatens the subsistence of the have-nots. 5) Food Stamps require expensive monitoring system to insure that they are used for the purpose they were intended; to determine the eligibility of the recipients, to assess the level of their disability, to devise a system of workfare, and still to continue to feed them in situations where they exchanged their Food Stamps for money and spent it on non-essentials. 6) Food Stamps are unfair because many freeloaders get free lunches in a system where there are no free lunches, which demoralizes and punishes the workers. 7) Food Stamps can be abused, embezzled, double-dipped, counterfeited, and dealt in, as is often the case with regular currency. 8) And finally, they stigmatize the recipients even more than the welfare cheques do. Only the agency, which cashes the welfare cheque, knows the name of the recipient whereas food stamps brand most of their users as freeloaders by any grocery clerk.

Secondly, the free food staples have nothing to do with Socialism or Communism. Socialism is a state-imposed religion. It is a violent doctrine, which does not leave a person alone, or permit him to define the parameters his own existence and his goals in life, whereas free food staples program does not do it. A person who is not on the market for anything should not be starved into working for money, so that he could just pay for his food. He has to work because naturally he cannot live without working. Although a person cannot live without working, he should be able to live without working for pay. This is what I mean by 'Freedom not to Work.'

To understand why the free food staples are not socialist or communist in origin, we must remind ourselves of the definition of our terms. The dictionary definition of 'free enterprise' is "freedom of private business to organize and operate for profit without interference by government." In broad sense of the word we all are entrepreneurs conducting one-person business operation. As such, to be free, we ought to keep government off our backs. 'Dictatorship' on the other hand is defined 'as a form of government in which absolute power is concentrated in a dictator or a small clique.' 'Ideology' is defined as a systematic body of concepts especially about human life or culture.'

Now to put these definitions into relationship with each other, ideology and dictatorship go hand in hand whereas free enterprise in its pure form is free of ideological coloration. Why so? The free enterprise reflects the factual state of human life, whereas the ideology reflects the idea not what life is but what it should be. Now, any government driven by an ideology needs dictatorial powers to impose its will on life as it is. You cannot have a government founded on an ideology *of any kind*, without resorting to dictatorship at the same time. Thus, I would have accused any ideologue of being pro-dictatorship, even if he were going to establish the Kingdom of Heaven here on earth. It is not only indoctrination with Communism that requires violent means under a dictatorship. Socialism, Christianity, Hinduism, Islam, et al. could also not get very far without bloodshed.

Scientific facts, based on self-evidence of what is natural, or based on a logical argumentation and inference drawn from true premises, cannot be considered to be ideological. Thus to say that one must breathe, or eat, or that body must work to digest food, or that we must work to bring food to our mouths, is to say that this is the way things are. On the other hand, to say that we *must not* be driven by greed of acquisition, or that *we must* love our neighbour, or worship no other idols but the one, which this or that church had chosen for us, or that we all must be equally wealthy, is ideological.

44

It is futile to try to change the human nature as it is. We may want to be equal to some idol above us, but we certainly do not want to be equal to the masses of people below our standards. And although we desire the opportunity to be successful we certainly do not wish everyone to follow our footsteps and be equally as successful. In a society free from ideology we are all equal in our desire to be superior to everyone else, i.e. we are all equal in our inequality. This is a healthy competition, which permits some people to reach the pinnacle of wealth, knowledge, power, popularity, etc.

Where does the word 'capitalism' fit into our deliberation? Capitalism is not a pure ideology, a religion, or a political system, but rather a product arising from an interaction of ideologically driven government (or corrupt government) and the free enterprise. It is like a colour red produced by interaction between magenta and yellow light waves. If magenta colour were to stand for 100% dictatorship and yellow for 100% free enterprise, the resulting shades of red, ranging from crimson, to deep red, to orange, to orange yellow would analogously stand for a variety of shades of capitalism. In this sense, the present food distribution system is capitalistic.

One hundred percent free enterprise could only be found in a democratic society, which is one hundred percent free of any ideological bias. Such a democratic society protects us from anyone invading our private and personal space. We do not have to listen to sermons and political speeches, watch or listen to certain programs on TV or radio, read propaganda leaflets, newspapers, or books. We are not forced to attend any pep rallies, recite Lord's Prayer and the articles of faith. We can refuse to accept help, treatment, or any kind of salvation offered to us. It does not creep under our skin or between our bed sheets. It does not try to indoctrinate us with some weird ideas, such as to love anything or anybody, to wear a constant grin on our face to prove that we are happy or to be more or less greedy, etc. It gives no hoot about woman's hair showing from under her scarf or whether the male assumes a missionary position in his procreative act.

Because the free democracy is free of the mission to indoctrinate, it is incongruous with dictatorship. To train a tiger to jump through the flaming hoop requires a gun, a whip, a chair, and a cage. This is a dictatorship, and the force is needed because it is unnatural for a wild beast to perform such an act of itself. A democracy accepts the human nature for what it is, including greed and avarice. To say that it is *natural* for people to be egocentric, greedy, etc., does not express any ideology, which would be the case if one said that they *should not* be that way.

Thus capitalism is a mixture of ideology and the free enterprise. It got its bad reputation from four sources: 1. the private enterprise seeking protection by a corrupt government against people's interference with its function, 2. accepting the human nature for what it is, with specific reference to the avarice and greed for profits, 3.the free enterprise functioning at its optimum in the atmosphere of free market practices, 4. maximizing its profit by avoiding the responsibility for damages to the environment and human health.

As to the first point, a corrupt government, guaranteeing a company free hand in exploiting the resources of its land, works for its own enrichment, neglects the welfare of its people and leads to insurrection. The cooperation between both of them produces unsavory kind of capitalism, the free enterprise carrying the blame.

As to the second point, greed for something, whether it is the greed for money (the avarice), or greed for fame, or love of god, is the most essential motivating factor, which drives people to accomplish a goal and make sense out of their lives. Without a goal, most people would have no purpose in life and no reason to be. 'What's in it for me' is not immoral but an integral part of human nature. All human acts are egocentric or else they would not take place. The payoff is always there in one form or another, whether it is entrance to the kingdom of heaven, smugness that one had done the right thing, freedom from guilt, a material reward, or expectation that a good turn will be reciprocated in times of need, to mention just a few.

As to the third point, under the free enterprise system, in a democratic and ideologically free society, a person should be free to sell anything he owns, his body, parts of his body including his organs, the usage of his physical and intellectual skills for whatsoever purposes. It is prostitution in the broad sense of the word. The evil comes from the government, like the one driven by the ideology of the work ethic, which forces a person to do it, in order to survive, the idea being that he who does not work in order to eat, shall not have money to pay for his food, and therefore shall not eat. This by itself produces a large gaping wound in the human dignity, and the specific embargo on organ trading is just a flimsy band-aid to cover the injury.

As to the last point, businesses do eventually face up to their responsibility when proven guilty in the courts of law, and do pay up.

WHAT FREE FOOD
STAPLES WOULD NOT DO

In the light of what was said above, free food staples not being ideological, are compatible with all forms of democratic governments. Unbridled free enterprise business practices can flourish under it. Thus one is free to choose between giving the neighbour a loaf of bread when he is hungry, or giving him stone instead, if he showed no money. If he asked for fish but refused to pay, one would be free to give him a poisonous snake instead, depending on what made sense to him at the moment.

Free food staples would not interfere in the process of productivity. Naturally, free people would be difficult to handle. If one called them "parasites" and then waved in front of them $100 bill, they might not wink an eye. They would not have to work for anyone if they didn't like him. One would have to be nice to them. To be nice to people is hard, I agree. But, if one wants to be productive one would have to overcome such obstacles. One would have to be persuasive, put on a mask of piety and altruism, and bite one's tongue when reasoning with uneducated and ignorant. Agreeably, this would be much harder task than saying: "Here is $10, take it or leave it! Next one please!"

Free food staples would not change the nature of employer/employee relationship. As before, one would negotiate the pay. If the work was unattractive, the pay offer might need to be higher. If one was not willing to work for the pay offered, and the employer could not afford to pay more, then he either would have to do the work himself, or give up on the project.

The free food staples would only strengthen the practices of the free enterprise but not undermine it. Making staples accessible to everyone free of charge and unconditionally could not be accomplished without the help of the free enterprise system, since it is the one which is capable of producing such food at affordable prices in required quantities.

There might be fear that eliminating work ethic by making food staples available unconditionally free of charge to everyone would create a situation in which no one would be available to do any job. Ergo, there might not even be anyone to administer the Plan. This fear, however, is without foundation.

For how and why would a scenario change with a free bag of flour? Let us consider the following: I walk out of the supermarket with a cart full of goods. Amongst them there are chocolate chip cookies, frosted cornflakes, a carton of Coke, for which I paid, and a bag of flour, a bottle of cooking oil and two dozen of eggs which were free of charge. Why would the world, as we know it, come to an end as the result of this? How would it come about that there would be no line-ups for a job to administer the food plan, which paid well? Why would even those people who believed that work was salutary and good for everyone, go into a catatonic stupor just because they got a bag of flour free of charge, after they paid for it by their food premium? And finally, why would a consumer in a consumer society, who was born to shop, and who was surrounded by fantastic variety of goods on the store's shelves, turn up his nose and say: "I have my bag of flour, what else do I need?

There would be nothing to prevent individuals from performing any type of work for no money. With free food staples everyone who worked would do so because he wanted to. At present, putting food on the table is the main driving force, but when survival is at stake, "wanting" as a motivating force has to be put on the back burner.

In general one would want to work to reach the set up goal of usefulness for oneself. Here are some parameters of one's usefulness, which under Free Food Staples for all, some people might find worthwhile to pursue:

1. To allow myself to be used by others, 2. To amuse oneself, 3. To assert one's superiority, 4. To clean up environment, 5. To collect and accumulate, 6. To create, 7. To delight in things, 8. To discover, 9. To escape boredom, 10. To express oneself, 11. To atone for one's sins, 12. To find god, 13. To find oneself, 14. To fight evil, 15. To get away from the dreary Canadian winters, 16. To get away from people, 17. To get paid, 18. To give other people pleasure, 19. To help, 20. To

invent, 21. To learn, 22. To lose oneself, 23. To manage things, 24. To manufacture things, 25. To organize things, 26. To play games, 27. To praise god, 28. To proselytize, 29. To punish, 30. To see justice done, 31. To seek adventures, 32. To seek contact with people, 33. To suffer, 34. To wield power, etc., etc, Whose business would it be to question their motivation, anyway?

WHO WANTS TO BECOME A MILLIONAIRE?

All roads lead to Rome and all political discussions lead to food. You can discuss wealth, power, fame, trade etc. but after a few hours your nature forces you to find something to eat. If you find the needed food the discussion continues while eating, if not it is highjacked by preoccupation with food. It is my contention that although we might be discussing wealth on the surface, it is sausages that dance in our heads. In reality no one wants to be wealthy just for wealth sake. Possessions might actually impede living. In reality what we want is the security and the power which wealth appears to bestow on us.

A realistic portrayal of the human nature can be found in Grimm's fairy tales, called "The three wishes:

"A woodcutter saved a tree, where the elf lived, and was in return rewarded with three wishes. Up to that time a plate of hot steaming soup was always waiting for him, when he came home in the evening. This time, however, after he told his wife about his good luck, she served both of them a glass of fine wine. "Nice," he said, smacking his lips. "But I wish I had a string of sausages to go with it, though…" (Not millions of dollars mind you, but a string of sausages!). Instantly he bit his tongue, but too late. Out of the air appeared the sausages. Thus contrary to what a corporate person would do, he thought of food first, and thus acted irrationally by wasting the first wish.

Now the lower part of the limbic region of his wife's brain kicked in, and in a fit of anger, she wished that the sausages stuck up her husband's nose. Here again she did not act in a businesslike fashion. She could have said: "My dear husband! There is no use crying over spilt milk. The first wish was wasted, let us fry the sausages, and have another glass of wine! Perhaps initially you should have wished to become a millionaire, but we still have two wishes left, and now we can compensate for it by wishing to become multibillionaires instead." However, she did not do this. True to her really human nature, she wasted her second wish on disfiguring her husband's face, as a punishment for his having foolishly wished for sausages.

This prompted the woodcutter's lower limbic region to kick in and he slipped into compassionate and loving mood. As a good corporate person he could have said to himself: "To be truly businesslike I must quest for financial gain. So, I must not waste my last wish on frivolity. I shall wish for trillions of dollars and as a multitrillionaire I will not only be able to pay for the plastic surgery on my nose, but I can also divorce my wife and marry someone much younger!"

Being truly human, however, he wasted his third and last wish by wishing that the sausages would leave his nose. And they did. The sausages were fried and husband and wife hugged each other tearfully, saying, "Maybe we'll be poor, but at least we'll be happy again."

The true human nature requires primarily a full stomach in order to be healthy and functioning at all. After that it demands a complete freedom to embark on the odyssey of one's life, steering each his own vessel to the port of his desire, even if his odyssey would not prove to be beneficial to a society or the corporations.

Our imagination is not any greater than that of the woodcutter. So, what is it that we really want? In my opinion, we want three things: to be in good health and have warm shelter and enough food to live on. (This could be provided by the premium-supported free food staples and shelter plan). Then we would like to be able to fulfill our immediate desire, to do something exciting, to reach for the stars, to have an adventure, to be involved in a project, to move and to interact, provided that our earthly possessions did not keep us chained too close to the ground. Thirdly and finally, we would want to have the security of being able to do this each day of our remaining lives. This is what the bag lady would do if she was given a few thousands dollars: she would have a decent meal, replace her plastic bags with canvass ones and stuff the rest into her bag as a security for the rainy days.

PREPAYMENT

It never ceases to amaze me how such simple, familiar, and mundane concept as "prepayment" could be so misconstrued, as to make it look like a futuristic term in need of being studied and "buttressed with real live data," requiring "the research to back it up," followed by discussion and evaluation whether it could ever be made "attainable."

Paying for things in advance (prepaying) is the way of commerce. It is as old as the monetary system itself. There is no other way! Each one of us is engaged in paying for things in advance all the time, without an exception. It needs no Ph.D. thesis to prove its existence. We cannot acquire anything without prepaying, i.e. paying for it first. Any other way of conducting business is a theft.

What is the difference between payment and prepayment? Essentially there is none, since both terms denote payment in advance. There is always a time interval between the payment (or a promise to pay) and actual possession of goods and services purchased.

When you pay for things, and take possession of them, or consume them within minutes of the purchase, then you pay for them. When you pay for thing in order to take possession or consume them days or months later, you prepay for them. Thus, if you attend a performance at the theater, and buy your ticket at the door, you are paying for it. If you bought your ticket six months in advance you prepaid for it.

We already enjoy the prepaid food plan, albeit only on individual and small groups level. Each time we go to the supermarket we prepay for food, which we will consume days and months later. If we attempt to consume any food inside of supermarket without having paid for it first, we run the risk of being charged with shoplifting.

We prepay for our food when we go for a buffet dinner. We prepay for our food six months in advance when we buy all-inclusive package tour. We prepay for our rent and board, for delivery of deep-frozen meats and vegetables, etc. These are real live data, based on experience. They speak loud and clear that prepaid food is not only "attainable" but has been with us from times immemorial, albeit on individual and groups level only.

The prepayment for goods and services in advance, and as a group, is much less expensive than paying for them individually, or at the time of their consumption. Subscription to theater performances and magazines is much cheaper when done years in advance, than it is when paying for a single performance, or a single issue a few minutes before. Group rates for life and health insurance are progressively lower with the increased number of the participants. Seen in this light the plan is not at all futuristic. Rather, it is as simple as saying: "If I can prepay (pay in advance) or subscribe for a vacation trip, can I also prepay (pay in advance) for my meals?" and "If I can prepay for my meals as an *individual*, can a group of us do the same thing *collectively*?" One does not need a degree to answer these questions in affirmative. If we can save money on food and do away with hunger, food banks, and soup kitchens; and put a few more dollars into the pockets of consumers, and thus stimulate economy and create more jobs, all at the same time, then *what are we waiting for*?

Having thus prepaid the food staples means that we had money to pay for it, i.e. that the money changed hands. It further means that the money one had was obtained from the three sources outlined previously in this book, one of which may have been selling oneself, one's labour, or something belonging to one for a price. In the end it means that we are buying into the lifelong supply of food staples in the same way as we buying into possessing our own house or other property.

Now, with this system in place, do people still have to work to eat? Putting it differently, do people have to pay again for the staples after having already paid for them at the time of prepayment? The answer, of course, is that this would be preposterous. No one pays twice for anything.

MEANING OF 'FREE'

The comprehension of the word 'free' does not fare any better than the comprehension of the word 'prepaid.' To say that something is free is a manner of speech. All food from whatever source is the result of some human interaction with nature (read work) and/or other humans. And no work is *ever* without the cost. How could food be free? It is free in the same sense as the air we breathe is free. We understand the usage of this term when we speak of numerous other things, which are free in our society.

If food did not grow of itself, we would never be able to make it grow. However, people involved in its cultivation, interact with nature and other people and demand payment. This interaction is even more visible in all medical procedures under National Health Plan. Consider the heart-transplant surgery! If the latter can be had for free, i.e. on the prepaid basis, upon having paid health insurance premium, why couldn't food be treated in the same manner?

The free food staples plan would make staples available free of charge to everyone on the retail level, upon payment on the wholesale level. In reality, it would be paid by each individual who had an income, calculated on a sliding scale. Also, to say that *no* work is *ever* without cost does not express universal truth. It is only valid if one subscribes to such an ideology. In a society free from ideology its meaning could be: If I do for you what you ask me to do, and say to you that it will cost you an arm and a leg, then the cost will be high. On the other hand, if I do it for you out of goodness of my heart, then the work will cost you nothing. Volunteers, homemakers and hobbyists work for free. It all depends on our definition of "work," "cost" and "free."

It is not the question of the free food somehow materializing from the thin air without the human effort. X-ray machines, CAT scan machine, all surgical instruments, hospital beds, etc. do not "somewhat materialize" under National Health Plan, even though health services are free. We are talking here about *prepaid health plan, prepaid maintenance of highways, prepaid elementary education and the prepaid military.*

Thus "free food" is not in reality free, but subscribed to or paid for in advance. One gets only what one prepaid for! If better cuts of meat are not designated as a *staple,* and are not prepaid for, one just doesn't get them no matter how hard one pleads his case.

Let me point out all the things considered to be free, but down deep in our unconscious we know full well that someone had to pay for it. I already mentioned the air we breathe. We know, that the air we breathe is not free. It does not fall from heavens. The pollution control costs money. The industries have to invest their capital into emission control; government has to have a large department of bureaucrats to enforce such controls. The air to some public buildings has to be pumped in, filtered, dehumidified and its temperature adjusted. All in all, it is costly to breathe. Each breath one takes is the result of interaction between humans and the nature and it costs money.

It follows that if we did not pay taxes we would not be able to breathe. The clean air is expensive. However, breathing is a vital human need and we do pay for it in taxes by helping the industries to reduce pollution. We could not accomplish it by paying premiums or prices. It is hard to imagine someone introducing a free breathing plan, like the one described below, analogous to the free food staples plan.

Paying breathing tax e.g. 1/100 cent per hour, is a small amount but in one day it would come to 0.24 cents and $0.87 cents annually. The instant that this would happen, the taxpayer would get up in arms and say that everyone had to take personal responsibility for their lives. He would not be willing to pay taxes and have some lazy sloth breathe for free while watching TV. There are no free breaths! People should not depend on the government for their breathing. Free breathing is preposterous. Breathefare (analogous to workfare) would be instituted; breathing vouchers issued and some people would be accused of irresponsibly breathing the air borrowed from the year 2,010. People who were unwilling to give back to the society what they took from it would be branded as social parasites and be equipped with chokers, their nostrils plugged with whistles and wheezers, conspicuous in public, and removable only when they went back to work and paid their free-air-taxes. In times of crises taxes might be cut to reduce budgetary deficit, resulting in increase of air pollution. Breathing saloons would spring up. The shortage of whistles would paralyze the social order, etc.

The present food distribution system ought to be treated the same way as we treat the air we breathe, or water we drink, or public washroom facilities we use. Thus although the air we breathe is free, it is being paid for with our taxes without irritating us with the knowledge of the fact.

Potable water is another example of something that costs a lot of money but which is free in our society. Drinking water fountains are ubiquitous in offices, fast-food restaurants, bars, public places, etc. Water is freely served in restaurant before meals. Potable water and water purification plant are one of the first items in humanitarian aid offered to a country struck by an ecological disaster. Not only the water is free but so are the machine-washed glasses and paper cups.

Why is it that we do not sell water as precious commodity, which in reality it is. The answer is that it is in the interest of public health *not to* commercialize it. To live we have to drink water. We do not want to see those who happen to be thirsty but insolvent or penniless at the moment, to drink from contaminated sources and cause the outbreak of enteric diseases.

Other free items in our society are the public washrooms with all their hot water, soap, towels and cleaning staff. To say that they are free does not mean that they somewhat materialized from heaven and that no one had to work to construct and to maintain them. They are expensive, but we are paying for them collectively, without protestations that some lazy sloth may use half the roll of a toilet paper, or use the toilet every half an hour, without paying his debt to society.

There is a good reason for all that. In Eastern Europe, in my younger years, when nature called, young people relieved themselves in the entrances to the apartment houses, or in the less frequented back alleys. One was able to find his way to the back alleys just by following one's nose. Prosecutions were rare and finding a person guilty of public mischief was impossible in the absence of the available public washrooms.

Hot water, soap, paper towels, toilet paper, the maintenance of plumbing and sewage disposal, keeping the premises clean and warm does not come in cheap. In Europe some public washrooms had coin-operated doors, or an attendant was sitting at the entrance, dispensing the paper and collecting donations.

Public washrooms are free, but we pay for them in one form or another. Each gasoline station, restaurant, office, public building, is mandated to have one for public use. All of this is in the interest of public health, environmental pollution, beautifying our highways and the city streets, and protecting each one of us from indecent exposure by others, using a pretext.

Air, water, and public washrooms are free in practice, but in reality prepaid for by our taxes. No one ever questions it. It is taken for granted. However there are hundreds of other items in our society that are also called 'free,' but are included in the price we pay for things. Examples are: serviettes, cutlery and the chairs to sit on when eating our meals in a restaurant; advertising in magazines, the entertainment we watch on television, health care we receive when ill, policemen responding to our 911 call, etc.

Although there are no free lunches, some lunches are free, when offered to prospective buyers in exchange for attending a seminar, or an exhibition, or a lecture. Free calculators and watches are given as incentive to buy more expensive items. Buying two of certain merchandize rewards one with the third one 'free of charge.'

In other words, they are free because *no money* changes hands at the time we avail ourselves of them. We know that in reality whatever is free was paid for and we are the ones who paid for it one way or another without having noticed it.

STAPLES

Now that we are in the clear what we mean by free, we must crystallize our understanding of what we mean by 'staples.' One would think that the word 'food staples' is understood by everyone to mean what it stands for. Not so. Were this the case no such questions, as the ones quoted below would have been asked in one of the discussion groups in which I took part: "Is carbonated water a staple? Spices? Ingredients for weight gain shakes? All vegetables? All fish? Cereal? High-fructose corn syrup? Baking powder? Cocoa? Grapes? Raisins? Cranberries?

Asking these questions betrayed a complete incomprehension by the questioner not only of the word 'staple,' but also of the word 'food.' Because, had he understood the word 'staple' he would not have wondered whether 'all fish, grapes, raisins, and cranberries' were included. Had he understood the word 'food,' he would not have included in it carbonated water, spices, and baking powder.

After being given a dictionary definitions of food staples as: "that food which forms a basic part of one's everyday diet," another debater came up with the following statement; "Another fundamental problem is that you haven't offered a simple definition which would include some items while excluding others. Strawberries *meet* your definition of a staple, as does asparagus."

My experience of debating issues on the Internet, albeit a frustrating one, taught me one thing: if a person asks stupid questions, then he is either himself stupid or hostile to the concept under discussion. In such a case he will demonstrate incomprehension of the entire issue, by showing lack of comprehension of single words.

Here is another definition of food staples: 'they are ingredients that go into the preparation of hundreds cooking and baking recipes. They could be eaten raw, cooked, and mixed in different proportions to crate a meal.' No one can avoid eating them in one form or another. In the end staple is anything one declares it to be; anything that money can buy; any product in sufficiently large supplies able to fill the market demands.

WHAT IS THE PREPAID
FOOD STAPLES PLAN?

Now that we have clarified the words 'free' and 'staples' let us combine them in the phrase Free Food Staples Plan and see what is meant by it. This Free Food Staples Plan, also referred to, as "Prepaid Food Staples Plan" or "Universal Compulsory Prepaid Food Staples Plan," or "Premium-supported Free Food Staples Plan" is the practical implementation of "Food for All" and "Food Security" enunciated by the World Food Summit held in Rome from Nov.13 to 17, 1996.

It is a plan in which every member of a society has unhindered, unconditional, constitutionally guaranteed access to the food staples, free of charge, i.e. free of any monetary transactions whatsoever on the retail level.

It is a system in which the electorate establishes a public agency, as a single payer, dealing with any private enterprises involved in a provision and distribution of staple foods for the entire country.

It is a Humanitarian Aid, which a country gives to itself, on a permanent basis, without being forced into it by major climatic, environmental, economical or political catastrophes, having learned its lesson from history that shortages of food lead to social unrest, revolution and wars.

It is a subscription to a program of providing staples to each subscriber for the duration or his/her life, and paid by monthly, quarterly, or yearly installments.

It is a trifling act, reminiscent of introduction of credit cards or direct payment method, whereby we derive considerable saving by rearranging the method of our payments and by this act alone, without any labour pains and without resorting to violence, cause our entire society to be born again.

BENEFICIAL SIDE EFFECTS OF
PREE FOOD STAPLES

Human dignity reestablished

Constitutionally guaranteed, unconditional access to free food staples creates circumstances in which human dignity can be re-established. This is made possible by the fact that no one is forced into meaningless for them activity, just to survive. It allows us the freedom to be rich or poor by our choice. It allows each and every person to define his own mission and purpose in life. This means that we shall not be programmed, brainwashed or indoctrinated against our will. We don't want to be pigeonholed in a job created for us. We are not born to play an _assigned_ role in a script written by politicians, church leaders, social workers or corporations. We have the inborn right to be what we want to be: a good guy, a benefactor, a do-gooder, a helper, creator, a manufacturer, an inventor, etc. or to be unproductive, unprofitable, deviant, irresponsible, crazy, stupid, unreasonable, a sloth, an alcoholic or a drug addict, by our own choosing. It is our life! It is below human dignity to be cast in concrete in any shape or form, be its name "sanity", "normalcy", or "doing penance for the original sin."

It bears repeating that human dignity does not consist in being something or somebody in particular; a president of the country, CEO of a corporation, a doctor, a lawyer, a teacher, or a janitor. The dignity lies in the freedom to choose and become what one wants to be. Free food staples would entirely eliminate _forcing_ people to work. People would work if they wanted to work, and be idle if they didn't want to. Why would they want to? Most of the time for money, but not to buy staples, but rather to buy fruits of other people's creative genius and labour, in fact, _any merchandise_ now on the market that remain after one subtracts from it such staple foods as flour, bread, oil, eggs, etc.

New social freedom and mobility

The access to free food staples would give a person the opportunity to say to himself: "Food staples are free for the taking in any grocery store in the land. I do not have to stay home to have three square meals a day and a roof over my head, because the Constitution guarantees my survival for lifetime, anywhere I choose to live. If I just want to philosophize about god, evolution, creation, but do not want anything else in life, then I am free to do so with impunity.

If I have a bright idea how to make a better mousetrap, I can entice on board qualified people, whose survival is also guaranteed by the Constitution, and who can work for nothing, in hope to share the profits with me, when they materialize. My wife had married me out of love and not as a meal ticket, and since she and my children also have the free access to food staples, it is not critical that I take on a brain-deadening job for minimum wages, requiring me to stay put in one place, to put food on the table. I may go to the University located in other parts of the country, work for a while there for nothing, establish connections, show them my creative potential, get a degree and perhaps get a job as an assistant professor, etc."

Monetary emasculation

Money is the circulating substance in the body of economy. It has the nature of its own, which cannot be altered or fixed. Analogy between circulation of water and money is befitting here. Like money, water has no measuring standards specific to it: one unit of water may mean a drop, a milliliter, a liter, a gallon, a puddle, a lake, or an ocean. In a similar fashion a dollar may be stretched or contracted to mean one cent or one grand. Both substances have no shape of their own but only mimic the containers they are in. They have no loyalty to their owner but gravitate toward the lower gradient. They can become polluted and breed all kinds of sharks and predatory creatures. Too much or too little of one or another can devastate our lives, but after learning to live with them they may be life sustaining.

We have reached a point where boarders between the economy and us become blurred. When sick, we wonder whether we suffer from physical, mental or economic disorder. To treat an illness we may be transfused with blood or given an injection of capital. A person may starve because he is insolvent or has no food to eat. At times we get confused about whether economy is a malignant growth on our backs or whether we ourselves are parasitic appendages on the body of economy. Consequently, economy may try to purge itself of us, or as a backlash we may try to shake economy off our backs.

In such a state of affairs we cannot enjoy a free and independent life. What is the solution? We must get the economy off our backs! We must set it free! How? By making our biological survival independent of circulation of money, but only dependent on nature. This can be accomplished by making free food staples available on a prepaid basis.

We should make economy stand on its own feet and accept responsibility for its own well-being. It should not be protected, nurtured and pampered by the governments, by favourable legislation and exemptions from prosecution for environmental pollution and safety violations. It should not receive handouts in form of subsidies, tax grants, business incentives, job training and job creation while people starve without dignity. Let us cultivate economy as if it were a milking cow, or a water tap, and turn it on and off as desired. Let us make it subservient to our needs. If necessary, let us sacrifice it for the benefit of humanity, but never sacrifice ourselves to keep it alive. Let it be at our beck and call but not the other way around. This accomplished, we will not only be free *not to work* (not to trade) in a philosophical sense, but also be able to exercise this freedom in achieving human dignity, without fearing for our lives.

A gun without bullets is a toy. An ideology, a political system, a set of ethics, without the power to impose it on other people, is a word play, a fiction, a fantasy, or just simply an entertainment. All ideas, all religious or secular ideologies, and all systems, which end with the suffix '-ism', fall into this category. Toying with these ideas is playing a game. Forcing others to play these games is a tyranny and dictatorship. Money becomes a tyrant when our government allows it to control our access to food staples. This renders our lives dependent not on availability of food, but on availability of money, employment, the state of economy, Dow-Jones Average, etc.

It follows that in order to emasculate money, to depose it as a tyrant preventing us to live in dignity, our subsistence has to become independent of it. Food has to come first and the economy, money and the performance of the stock market, second. The tiger has to be made edentulous. The sting has to be taken out of a bee, venom out of the snake, teeth and the claws out of a tiger, virulence out of a disease, the ability and the opportunity to commit a crime out of ordinary people, the ability to produce weapons of mass destruction out of a political system, the guns out of the hands of the violent criminals. This accomplished the threat to our well-being will be rendered harmless. In the same vein, the mandate that one *has to* work for his subsistence has to be taken out of the social system, to free ourselves from the dictatorship of money and the work ethic, without destroying monetarism and the free enterprise.

Freedom of individual not to work

Only a person in prison is free not to work. The rest of us are forced to look after our health and welfare, but the inmate cannot be forced to do anything. His guards don't get free food. They *have to* work for it! But *he* is free from this obligation. He made a 'contribution' to society. He raped, killed, kidnapped, stole, vandalized etc., therefore he earned his keep. He cannot be tortured or starved, even if he were of Somali origin. Such a system is grossly unfair.

Free staples would emasculate money and allow us to exercise our free will, to work or not to work, to sin or not to sin. It seems that freedom to choose is the essence of Christianity. No person can claim being virtuous if such virtue is imposed on him by force or when it is performed automatically, in a robot-like fashion. When it comes to the choice of doing evil to stay alive, and doing good but to die in the process, I believe that doing evil will win most of the time.

Free staples would excuse the state from its duty to create the "Workers' Paradise" for the working class of people (in reality the Workers' Hell) and leave it up to each individual worker and non-worker, to create his own style of life, his personal heaven or hell.

Work ethic redefined

The work ethic in the era of free food staples would be redefined as follows: He who does not work *shall eat to his heart's content,* but shall have no money to exchange for goods produced by the effort of others. He will not be able to enjoy collecting, accumulating or bartering goods that were not obtained in the sweat of his own labour or ingenuity. He will be unable to acquire goods which only money can buy, without paying for them first.

Freedom to work for no monetary reward

In our democratic society, although we are equal in many ways, we are not equal in regard to freedom to choose whether we want to work for money or just out of curiosity, or for experience. Availability of free staples would make the retroactive pay a reality, which again would unburden the free enterprise from paying each worker a profit from the borrowed venture capital, before realizing such profit itself. As of now the proactive pay is mandated by the government, the rationale being that every employee needed sustenance whether his company realized any profits or not. If the company could not borrow more money and was not doing well it could go bankrupt and in reality the taxpayer would have to absorb all the losses. Free food staples would permit a person to work for reduced wages or no wages at all. A retroactive pay (or bonus) would be a bulwark against inflation.

Having freed a person from the necessity to put food on the table, the free staples would lead to the concept of *voluntary* activities. The word *voluntary,* which is frequently in use at the present time, exposes the fact that some activities are chosen by

69

the volunteer himself (like running for cancer, canvassing for polio, or chauffeuring cancer victims to the clinic) and which are not paid for, in contradistinction to involuntary ones, which a person is forced to do for pay.

How would unpaid volunteers be distinguished from those who are paid? There would be no distinction between them. To work under free staples plan would mean that one had chosen to work of his own volition to pursue his/her brand of happiness. It would mean that putting food on the table was not the impelling force behind it. It would mean that he wanted to enjoy life, have fun, achieve, create, learn, experience, have contact with other people and have access to their creative output. Money would still be a strong motivating force. In reality, since everyone who worked was free to choose whether he wanted to work or not, the distinction between them on grounds of volunteerism would be redundant and meaningless.

No need for job security

Job security as it is practiced now is more like a prison without which one could not live. Being pigeonholed in one job cripples one's growth, and saps one's strength and energy. It is necessary only because food is necessary for sustenance.

Work and money are not synonymous concepts. Each of them requires different approach for its resolution. They can coexist independent of each other. Simplifying and separating them permits us to define employment/unemployment in terms of one or the other, and in this definition lies its resolution. When unemployment is defined in terms of the job scarcity, the solution to it would be obvious: treat jobs as a commodity and put a price on it. The greater demand for jobs and the longer line-ups, the higher the price. Create jobs until the market is saturated with them. Charge for each job what the market can bear. Make jobs so expensive to get that only affluent could afford to work. The poor would have no choice but to embark on homemade jobs. Thus the unemployment issue would be disposed of.

On the other hand, if it is *money* and not work that mattered, then the answer to it is also very simple: find a way of improving

70

the monetary circulation in such a way that everyone would get a trickle of it coming his way, while bypassing the condition of having to work for it. There have never been labour strikes triggered by the company increasing hourly wages while reducing the working hours. It is always money and not work that matters when dealing with employment/unemployment question.

The obsolescence of 'making a living' concept

With free staples, "making a living" and "job security" as concepts would go out of the window. To work would mean: to take part in a project, whether of one's own invention or chosen by others, whether commercially viable or of questionable value, whether remunerated or not, whether backbreaking or a cinch.

No increased unemployment

Free food staples would do away with unemployment. At present this term is applied to those who are in receipt of Unemployment (Employment) Insurance. These are the people who want to work but don't have jobs. With the availability of free staples the unemployment or employment insurance would have no reason to exist. There would not be employed and unemployed, but rather those involved in a project, those who had just completed and are on the lookout for another project, and those leisurely people capable of enjoying their existence without any projects.

As of now employment is in essence a convoluted way to feed people. Once the political system had subscribed to the dictum that "there are no free lunches" it became incumbent on the government to see to it that money reached each individual on a regular basis, either through job creation or social assistance. It was not up to the private enterprise to take care of people's needs. The free staples would make job creation redundant. However, there would be plenty of things to do and things would be done and everyone would be busy doing his own thing. Availability of jobs would be a byproduct of manufacture of goods and provision of services.

Getting government off our backs

Only in a society run by a government free of any ideology can the enterprise be private and free. For greater efficiency, an enterprise must be free of government interference and free of obligation to do the job of running the country. Just because, as an entrepreneur, I organize the production of a better mousetrap I should not be burdened with responsibility to take care of my employees' health, their teeth, vacations, disability, retirement pension, maternity leave, or what have you.

A government which indoctrinates its members with the idea that they must suffer by working in the sweat of their brow and do the biblical penance for the original sin committed by Adam in the Garden of Eden, is the government which penalizes them by starving them into employment. For this reason it is bound to be forever on the backs of those it governs, and on the back of the supposedly free enterprise, prodding it to create more jobs and to pay to its employee's better living wages.

Such a government cannot be anything else but violent. It goes with the turf. For what is not valued is discarded, destroyed, quarantined, if it does not perish on its own. During the Inquisition the sinful human body was thrown into the fire to save the valuable soul. During the holocaust the people of 'no value' were thrown into the gas furnaces. Serbs in former Yugoslavia cleansed themselves of Croats and Muslims, who were of no value to them. In United States 2 million peoples are behind the bars at the present time, most of whom on drug related charges, because their presence in the society is not valued. Some of them just smoked marihuana, which was not good for their health, and the government, being its brother's keeper, put them in jail to save them from themselves.

Human dignity is not something malleable in one's hands, a subject of cleansing it of these or those undesirable traits. This is exactly what the Catholic Church had done in response to Pico dela Mirandola treatise on the dignity of men. He was charged

72

with heresy and would have been burned at the stake had he not sought refuge in Paris.

Prepaid staples open barriers to progress

In the light of the above statements, one can see how free food staples would remove the barriers to progress. We all know e.g. that solar energy is inexhaustible, renewable and clean. We have not developed it commercially, because it is uneconomical. It is more profitable to derive our energy needs from nuclear fission, coal, oil and gas. Why? Because these industries create jobs, and in order to put food on the table, people find employment there, which relieves the governments of the burden to feed them.

Governments distort the real prices of these products by hiding the costs of cleaning up the pollution, tax concessions, and subsidies they give to companies. Oil companies pretend that they pay the penalties for cleaning up the oil spills, but in reality all the money comes from the taxpayer's or car owners pocket. Oil companies don't print money!

With free food staples it would be possible for everyone to disregard the question of money and pursue such unremunerative activities as: enjoying leisurely existence, curios inquiry, gaining more knowledge, relief of boredom, association with interesting people, loving one's neighbour, helping environment, etc.

It would encourage greater degree of entrepreneurship and development in arts, discoveries and inventions. Everyone would become entrepreneur while at the same time being free of the responsibility of taking care of the social security of other entrepreneurs. The private enterprise would thus be more able to concentrate on providing goods and services of high quality and at competitive prices. The free private enterprise would become unbridled and free to 'exploit' anyone and everyone, by paying low wages or no wages at all, by putting no limits on working hours or making the workplace safe for its workers.

73

Exploitation made impossible

Free staples would make exploitation of one individual by another impossible in reality, since whoever is free not to work to put food on the table cannot be exploited by being forced to work. Every worker from the old system would thus become a willing participant in the new system, a new breed of volunteers, who either is not getting paid at all, or getting paid any wages agreed upon, concurrently or retroactively.

Development of other parts of the brain

With the labour-saving arrangement provided by the free staples permitting a person not to waste his time putting food on the table, more free time would to be available to develop other parts of his brain, variously referred to as: psychic powers, clairvoyance, astral travel, instant knowledge sans computers, etc. Our present educational system is geared mainly to job training. It does not prepare one for greater appreciation of life, fulfillment, pursuit of happiness and achievement of lofty goals. It rather prepares us for a paying job, which would permit us to put food on the table.

The present school-knowledge, which one obtains in this fashion, is of the kind that can be translated into binary language, suitable for computer programming. Ability or talent to obtain knowledge by routine or habit, rather than by thinking and trying to understand it is frowned upon. Actually one would fail the grade if one were unable to show the teacher the reasoning used in arriving at a correct answer.

A case in point is Indian-born Miss Shakuntala Devi, who at a demonstration given in Ottawa, Canada, in 1974 went head-to-head against such computers as Univac, IBM and Burroughs— and won. As described in the 'Globe and Mail' she multiplied 20-digit number by another 20-digit number and came up with the answer in the blink of an eye. She worked out in her head the cube root of a 29-digit number in about six seconds, established a record for 4th roots consisting of 32 digits, in three seconds; gave the cube root of 78,402,752 as 428. When she was asked to divide 22 by 7 she replied by repeating a decimal answer: 3.142857142857, etc., etc.

According to the article she started doing it when she was 3, traveled around the world for 20 years demonstrating her talents to mathematicians and computer experts, and was unable to explain how she did it. She said that she did not calculate the computation in her head but merely concentrated on the problem and the answer appeared.

The question is: could such talents be developed through special training by repeated exposure to a mathematical problem, encouraging the person to come up with the first thing that instantaneously flashed in his mind, exposing him to correct answer, doing it repeatedly with always different numbers, while monitoring the progress of coming closer and closer to a correct answer. This is the way golfers and sharpshooters train their brains; not by reasoning and understanding, but rather by practice and sending the message to the brain how close they were to hitting the target.

There are other 'wild' talents besides 'instant calculating,' pertaining to the mind-over-matter training, which could become ordinary abilities of the future men and women if only they had the labour-saving luxury of the free food staples.

Establishment of a sharing society

To force people to be sharing is a socialist concept and requires violent means for its implementation. There are a number of arguments on how to go about doing it but the key is to be found in a society that regards sharing to be of paramount importance. We are talking here about sharing food rather than sharing of money, which we already do each time we buy something, pay an insurance premium, buy into publicly owned company, or pay federal, state/provincial, or municipal taxes. We share the money willingly because it gives us something in return.

However, we regard sharing money to be of paramount importance _only_ when we ourselves are included into the pool of beneficiaries of such a sharing. We resent sharing things, if it is only for the benefit of others, but ourselves excluded. Thus we resent paying taxes in order to financially support the so-called unemployed poor, or to enable senior citizens to receive their Old Age pension, while we are disqualified to receive any of it, on grounds that our income is too high. This is unfair and discriminatory against the wealthy.

Were we to leave out the self-interest from any form of sharing, no casinos or lotteries could ever survive. If e.g. someone like Bill Gates, whose wealth is valued in billions of dollars, would hold a jackpot ticket for $10 millions, and be denied his windfall on grounds that, being a multi-billionaire already he would neither need it nor feel the difference if he didn't get it, then only the poor would buy the lottery tickets and in the end the jackpot would run dry.

By the same token, premium-supported universal plan for anything, be it shelter, prescription drugs, food staples, army surplus clothing, basic transportation, etc. would not be resented, if every member of a society could avail himself free and unconditionally of the said shelter, drugs, staples, clothing, and basic transportation.

Capitalizing on the aforementioned insight, and realizing that giving without receiving is an irrational act, the premium-supported universal free food staples plan appears to be in a position to instantaneously convert our non-caring and non-sharing society into its opposite. As a matter of fact it would kill three birds with one stroke. It would benefit each individual, it would transform the society into caring and sharing one, and at the same time it would eliminate hunger from our midst.

No need for charity

On cursory examination the free food staples would appear to be socialist or religious in origin. This would be the case if the plan had ideological underpinnings. If e.g. it were based on Matthew 25:34: "For I was hungry and you fed me; I was thirsty and you gave me water; I was a stranger and you invited me into your homes; naked and you clothed me; sick and in prison and you visited me" then indeed it would be either Christianity or

Socialism. As such it would require dictatorship to implement it and to reform human nature.

Appeal to charity is an attempt to take care of peoples needs by appealing to their good will and their charitable sentiment. However, charity is not natural. Those who have nothing appear to be charitable because having nothing they are only too willing to share this nothing with others. It is much harder to be chartable if one possessed little and was in need of charity himself. For the well-to-do it is easy to give that which one is ready to throw away, what one does not need, and what no one is willing to take from him without being paid for this service. The most profitable way to be charitable is when one gets in return more than what one gives away as charity.

St Matthew's appeal to feeding the hungry, giving water to the thirsty, and clothing the naked, requires the transformation of human nature. Using the whip, the gun, and the chair, a person can be trained to be charitable. It takes strong church with its weekly sermons, and dictatorial government to keep him in check and to keep reinforcing the training on the daily basis. The problem is that once the person is well trained in charity, he cannot pass this acquired trait to the next generation through hereditary transmission.

Free food staples would dispense with charities, because they would no longer be needed. Conversely, feeding the hungry with the free staples would be so easy and painless that one actually might become naturally more charitable under the circumstances.

Free food staples more convenient and cheaper

In the proposed free food staples plan one is simply prepaying for those food staples that are essential for one's everyday subsistence. This means that one is using his hard currency, whether he worked for it or not. One would do it because when the entire nation constitutes an insurance group it is much cheaper. Secondly, it is more convenient. How much money would one save on food, if 30 million Canadians subscribed to food staples as a group!

While giving a person welfare money so that he could buy himself something to eat, and the money is borrowed, one pays the interest on it, which eventually may exceed the amount of welfare. In other words, to give welfare to the poor one is compelled to give welfare to the lender. Because of the fluctuating nature of the interest rates, the value of the dollar and the inflationary nature of food prices, giving money may become unaffordable proposition. Further, with the introduction of the workfare, additional sum of money has to be spent on job creation. Also if the welfare recipient spends all his money on tobacco, alcohol and drugs, additional funds must be made available to nurse him into health or keep him alive in prison, hospital, or feed him via food banks etc.

No need for tax increase

With retroactive pay there would never be a need to increase taxes. Goods and services cost nothing until they are sold or until money from taxes is in the till. Feeding people via jobs is an expensive proposition and it is at the bottom of our present runaway taxation system. Not being permitted to eat without having a job or money can be likened to not being permitted to eat unless one had spoon and fork. There may be plenty of food in the country but people would be bound to starve if they had no money to buy that food for themselves, or analogously did not have the prescribed spoon to eat with. Furthermore, food may cost a small fraction of what job creation or manufacture of cutlery would cost.

As a matter of fact, free food staples would have no need of taxes as the plan would be self-contained, self-supporting, independent of jobs, and paid with hard currency in advance. For that matter all projects in a country could be supported by premiums: health care, shelter, education, transportation and clothing. There could even be, job-creation-premium, government organization premium, and defense premium as there are now life insurance and a fire insurance premium. The price would be set on everything else. There would be no distribution of wealth.

The advantage of handling social needs by prices and premiums is psychologically better than handling them by taxes because we know what we are paying for. If the society consumes greater amounts of food staples than the collected premiums are able to pay for, then understandably the amounts of premiums would have to be increased.

Taxpayer's resentment removed

Every vendor realizes some profit on selling his merchandise. He may use his profits for some nefarious purposes, but as long as the merchandise, which we buy, suits our needs, we don't mind. The same would apply to our prepayment for food staples and shelter. Why would we be resentful that the "profit" or "surplus" from it would feed and house some sloth, if all we are doing is buying *ourselves* the privilege to have a free access to staple foods and shelter?

Resentment to pay taxes makes as little sense as the resentment to pay premiums or prices. To be alive one must have in one's chest a pulsating heart to keep blood in a steady circulation. If the body demands greater supply of blood the heart must pulsate faster. Heart's resentment of having to work harder is irrelevant to life. It beats to keep person alive and, being a servant it has no power to mandate that some of its energy must not be frivolously spent playing golf or jogging.

Analogously, each member of a society is a little pulsating pump putting money into circulation. Just as it is impossible to stop the heart from beating and to stay alive at the same time, it is impossible to be a member of a society and not keep that society alive by pumping some money into its circulation. The resentment of each little money-pump that its money would be channeled into this and not that collateral branch of the circulation is irrelevant to the system. Each monetary transaction is like one pulse. It is called by various names: a tax, a premium or a price. Without the society being alive all those little money-circulating pumps could not be functioning, and without them the society could not live.

There exist hereditary resentment of giving someone something for nothing. When this question comes up, another one automatically springs into action: Where is the money going to come from? Who is going to pay for it? In what form is this payment going to be extracted from me? There exists an innate fear that "sponsors" and "sob-mongers for the needy" will grab and redistribute one's rightfully earned wealth. Naturally, they are vehemently opposed to any plan, which would enslave them or sacrifice them for the sake of others in the name of some altruistic doctrine. Others scream in horror: "Enough of taxation is enough! Are the taxpayers ever going to wake up and say emphatically 'enough is enough'? This continual bite on our pocket, this continuous tax grab must come to an end."

When is a tax not a tax, and how is one going to make up for sloths that don't/can't/won't earn money to pay taxes? One must realize that it makes no difference whether one pays taxes, premiums or prices; one cannot live without changing money in one form or another, and in addition, one has no control what the recipient does with his money. No matter what one pays, paying he must, and no matter how much he resents supporting sloths he ends up supporting them, even if he did not pay one penny in taxes, but paid price for everything as he went along. The following example should make it clear:

The price one pays e.g. for a car pays off hundreds of thousands people involved in its realization, from mining prospecting to mining, to iron smelting, transportation, to car designing, manufacturing, selling, etc. It pays the CEO's salary and bonuses; it pays the car dealers and stockbrokers, the janitors, the electricians, the gardeners, the truck drivers, and the cleaning staff. Now, each working person receives living wages, with which he supports his relatives and dependents. Each family of the working person may have one or two sloths, whom he chooses to directly support, but whom in reality we indirectly but unconsciously support by paying the price for a car. Thus every time we make a purchase we make a small contribution towards the support of all those cloths. We cannot escape this fact, and even being aware of this fact we still have no other choice than to go ahead with our purchases.

The present taxation system is psychologically unsound and fraught with many obstacles, the natural greed and possessiveness being the most important among them. Possessiveness is the natural quality of the mind, which makes us lay claim on everything we put our hands on. Give a child a candy and there is no problem. He will love you for it. However, give him ten candies and try to induce him to keep only two for himself, *but* share the remaining eight with others, and you will earn the reputation of being a meanie. All ten candies are naturally and inseparably his! Analogously, pay a person $1,000 an hour for his services, and he will grab it and instantly feel that he had earned it. Then try to pry from him $100 back to give it to the poor, and he will scream to high heavens: "Socialism! It is my money! I worked hard for it. Let freeloaders get off their butts and go to work!"

This possessiveness, not only of money but also of power, of property, of other people (as in marriage, or a dictatorship) is so strong that often it is impossible to separate the two without killing the possessor or the object of their possession. It is the closest thing to the holy matrimony where: "What God has joined together no man can put asunder." How then, under the circumstances, can one make money trickle down to the consumer so that he also could be empowered?

It is futile to try to change human nature; one has no choice but to live with it. Because people are greedy and possessive, one ought not to allow them to lay their hands on too much, so that later one would not have to pry a portion of it back. This means: *abolish all the taxes*, as being contrary to human nature! If a worker earns $10/h, make him happy by allowing him to keep it all. This is psychologically sounder than having him earn $25/h and then taking $15 back in taxes. Tax instead the employer and his automated appliances, robots, and computers. In this fashion you will bypass human greed and possessiveness and will be able to share the wealth, which these artificial slaves produce.

Paying the price seems to be most appealing to all of us, because we are free to pay it if we can afford it, and because we believe that we know what we are getting for it. In reality what we are getting is only tantamount to a consolation price. The situation is worse than with paying taxes, since the vendor is absolutely unaccountable for what he does with his profits. A government official cannot get off the hook that easy. To pay the price, however, is the most expensive way to acquire goods.

Acquisition of goods by paying premiums is more economical but we must submit to the rule of a collective, if we are to benefit from the low prices. A group of people decides to buy goods and services in bulk, wholesale. The more people participate the cheaper it becomes, whether we talk about HMO, car insurance, subscription to magazines, a delivery of deep freezer foods, the price of flight tickets, or belonging to the Price Club. Here again, we delude ourselves by the notion that we know what we are getting for our money.

The cheapest way to acquire goods and services is through paying taxes, which in essence is the same as paying premiums and prices, except that everyone in the country must pay it, and what we get for our money is absolutely impossible to obtain in any other way. There is for instance no way that one individual or a group of individuals, no matter how wealthy, could build, equip and maintain an army, air force or navy.

What the taxpayer resents most is paying for what he believes does not benefit him personally. An example is Old Age Security in Canada. It is a measly sum of $4,690 a year, which is clawed back from those whose income exceeds $53,000 a year. The same applies to the pension supplements, age amounts, tax on property and sales credits for seniors. He is paying taxes but other people reap the benefits thereof. This offends his egalitarian principles. It is just as unfair as it would be if he purchased a lottery ticket for one dollar and was prevented from collecting the prize of e.g. $1,000 because he was a millionaire and did not need it. The taxpayer resents feeding everybody else, by having his money forcibly taken away from him in taxes and still having to feed himself and his family afterwards.

In reality we *do know* what we are getting for our taxes but don't have the slightest idea what the vendor does with our prices. Apart from the military, we get government organization with all of its branches, construction and maintenance of highways, environmental protection, foreign representation, public education, health and welfare, maintenance of law and order, judicial and penal system, etc., etc. Without taxes it would be impossible to constructs even one stealth bomber, or one aircraft carrier, just by relying solely on voluntary donations.

What is necessary to convert taxes into prices is the consolation gift. If the government was in the habit of giving out precious gifts of ever increasing value for each amount of taxes collected, and if those gifts were manufactured strictly for the government, and not obtainable from anywhere else, then conceivably the taxpayer as a buyer would console himself with his purchases, forget that he was paying taxes, and not resent the government making huge profits on him and spending them frivolously.

Some people spend hundreds of dollars on lottery tickets every week but they do not resent that some freeloader will reap a benefit from it. Well, some gamblers are even ready to give the shirt off their backs for the opportunity to win the jackpot.

A person, paying food premiums, would find the system convenient and affordable, and at the same time giving him peace of mind that, no matter how bankrupt he would end up, he could always go on living without being humiliated by workfare, assessment of his ability to work, or trying to defend himself against the accusation of being lazy and a social parasite.

He would not need to become a do-gooder, a born-again Christian, a humanitarian, a benefactor, or an altruist. His premium would pay only for *his own* food staples, but at the same time benefit those without an income. Availability of free staples would bypass the resentment of the taxpayer because it would not be based on taxes but on food premiums, which everyone would pay.

To those resenting paying taxes it would be a dream come true. Everyone would be the beneficiary of the plan. Taxes could be abolished, redistribution of wealth stopped, money would not be pushed on the poor to make them wealthy. The preoccupation with job creation would be put on the back burner and the slavery would end. The rich would not be impoverished by the seizure of their earnings, children would be well fed, fathers would not be forced to work to feed them, no one would go hungry, and the size of the government could be reduced.

An argument can be made that the payment of the food staples premium would be compulsory whereas any other private insurance does not compel one to be part of its program. This however is not always the case. One is not able, for instance, to get a permit to drive a car unless one takes out public liability insurance. The taxpayer does not want to pay higher taxes to take care of people disabled in a car accident caused by the drivers who exercised their freedom to refuse to be compelled to be part of the program. One is compelled to take out liability insurance not for one's own good but for the good of all the taxpayers.

The same applies to all kinds of insurance schemes: health, fires, etc. They benefit us and it is of no concern to us that others benefit also. Therefore, we would not resent anyone receiving free food, whether from food banks or regular food outlets, if we could do the same without being discriminated against.

Disappearance of social classes

We supposedly live in a classless society in which titles denoting aristocratic background are not accepted unless they form the middle part of our names. The dignity of occupation goes along with hourly wages and fringe benefits; the higher the more dignifying.

Often repeated cliché in many discussions is that "Rich are getting richer and the poor are getting poorer." In absolute terms we are all wealthy to a greater or lesser degree. The sum total of Bill Gates's wealth can be estimated at $60 billions, or thereabouts. The wealth of a bag lady may not exceed $100. He is rich and she is poor. The rest of us fall somewhere in-between, but closer to the bag lady. Thus poverty is a relative concept and should be separated from hunger, which is not 100% correlated with it.

Now, does the bag lady really want to be wealthy? Suppose that, for the sake of an argument, we increased her wealth ten-thousand-fold and made her into millionaires. However, to accomplish this we would not give her cash, but only goods that are useless to her personally, but worth one million dollars on the free market, e.g. one of Picasso's paintings. How quickly would she get rid of her wealth? I would venture a guess that she would refuse the proffered Picasso painting and say: "One bird in the hand is worth two in the bush. The picture may be worth $100 millions but being a bag lady, I probably would be starved into giving it up for nothing, before I could even get a bite to eat. I don't want any headaches! Just give me $10,000 in cash and keep the change."

And, what would we do if suddenly an obscene amount of wealth were thrust upon us in similar manner? Supposed that we were told: "The Windsor Castle, or the Empire State Building, or the Taj Mahal were yours for the taking." Or better still: "As of today, you are Bill Gates, and all his valuable possessions and holdings in various companies, of estimated value of $60 billion are yours." Would we really want his wealth, or would we rather say: "Just give us $100 million in cash and keep the change"?

People are motivated by greed but not primarily for money, but for food and food security. The greed for money would be dramatically reduced if money was deprived of its power to force us to do things, as described previously. Hungry people have sausages dancing in their heads and not financial gain. There are 3 million hungry Canadians who rely on food banks. Foraging for food leaves them with no time to "pursue greed and acquisition."

The essential difference between the poor and the rich is not fancy clothes, gold chains, fast cars and large estates, but the fact that one is *hungry and has to work* and the other is *not hungry and if he works, he chooses to.* The wealthy are defined as those who by virtue of their wealth enjoy the full freedom to work or not to work, and if working, are free to choose only those types of work that are meaningful, enjoyable and fulfilling to them.

Under the free food staples social classes would disappear. The wealthy would be redefined in terms of objects they collected, which by their high value would be out of reach of the poor. They would collect for example: real estates, antique cars, racehorses, objects of art, etc. The poor could also be collectors, but of smaller things, e.g.: coins, stamps, buttons, shoes, etc.

However, both groups being beneficiaries of free food staples would not have to work and also have no power to force others to work for them. Thus the distinction between rich and poor would become blurred.

Maintenance of the present system creates social class divisions and breeds resentment between those who deserve to be fed and those who are unworthy of it, between those who pay and those who receive the benefits, and between those who pass judgment and those who are judged.

As of now two people, a prince and the pauper, wearing dirty clothes and cleaning the horse's stable, are on the surface indistinguishable from each other until one addressed the question which of them had to do this kind of work for living. Finding that one of them is a royal prince in love with horses and the other is just an average Joe, tells us who is who. The free food staples would make it impossible to tell.

Protection of the environment

At present a short-term benefit to human survival holds sway over protecting of the endangered species or saving the rain forests. A starving person would probably kill a whooping crane or a spotted owl for food even if to his knowledge they were the last representatives of their species on earth.

For if I am starving, or am forced to do stultifying menial jobs to subsist, I would rather opt out for a high-paying, sophisticated, and gratifying job, even at the price of destroying my environment. If the only way in which I can feed my family were by occupying the position of armed personnel guarding the food-warehouses, then according to my job description I would have to regretfully shoot the starving people trying to invade it. If the lack of medical attention would cause me to die at an early age, but the lack of food will definitely accomplish the same in a few weeks, then I would rather eat and put up with the poor health and face the death when it comes. Food would always come in first.

Since there would be no pressing necessity to create jobs to feed the hungry, and since a person would be free to refuse to work on the projects, considered by him to be harmful to himself, to the environment and to the endangered species, all three of them would benefit considerably from the availability of the free staples. It would protect the environment from pollution and destruction by doing away with the necessity of job-creation. Rare species of animals would survive, since the job of killing them would not be required to make a living.

Dissolution of political parties

With free staples there would be no need for government, as we know it. By the same token free democratic elections every so many years would be grossly superfluous. Political parties would dissolve themselves, not having any platform on which to run to be elected. There would be no promises with which they could bribe the electorate, no budgetary deficits, no job creation, no spending, no increases in social safety net, no environmental concerns, no wars to fight, no enforcement of human rights and no interference in private lives of its citizens. A country that is well fed, healthy, warm, educated and free to pursue its goal of happiness would not require any changes instituted by politicians.

For of what great benefit to the electorate would be the promise e.g. to reduce taxes? What they would be saying in fact would be this: since you don't know what specific purpose your tax-dollar is used for, we will reduce your taxes and allow you to have more money in your pocket to spend on prices of goods. This gesture on their part, however, would only have the effect of keeping the electorate even deeper in the dark. Paying e.g. $80,000 for Mercedes is not in any way different than paying the same amount in taxes, with exception that in the first instance one gets a consolation price in the form of new Mercedes. The rest of it remains the same. One does not know what the money paid for the car will be used for. In addition, in contradistinction to taxes, the downside of paying the price is that the car dealer cannot be held accountable, whereas the public officials are constantly being scrutinized.

Reduction of the crime rate

It is said that "devil will find work for idle hands." Would 'not working for living' be conducive to our spiraling down into the sin of idleness? Just the opposite would appear to be the truth. Working for living is frequently a mandate to do evil. Under the present system it is the sinner who is the fittest to survive. Not all work is ennobling and redeeming and not all work is for the good. Most of the evil we are asked to do is justifiable by the social imperatives. Some are undertaken in self-defense, some for peace, some for prevention of even greater evil, some in the name of God, or a Sovereign.

Man is neither good nor bad, but a social structure in which he lives, can make him act predictably evil. We live in a society where one's survival is dependent on having money for food staples. Selling oneself, one's service, or something one owns usually generates this money. In an atmosphere of struggle for survival, a man becomes a wolf to his fellow-man (lat. "Homo homini lupus"). By allowing himself to be hired to perform substantially remunerative work, one is essentially entering the services of evil.

The present system of food distribution does not allow us to discriminate between good and evil. We all are carrying out orders issued by our superiors, which are often justified by economic necessity. We do it for the privilege of making living and staying alive. We are not evil by nature but by our religion and culture.

To have free unconditional access to food staples would change the human behaviour in the way that even the great religions of the world could never have dreamed of. For one thing, the incidence of crime would be reduced, at least as it relates to the shoplifting or stealing of food. Free food staples would make it unnecessary for a person to do evil in order to eat. It was reported on TV that a person in California received a life sentence for stealing a slice of pizza from children. Mandatory life sentence applied there because this was his third felony offense. It is reasonable to assume that some other crimes are also committed for the purpose of biological survival.

Decrease in jail population

Each of us carries a quadruple burden on our shoulders: 1. We are forced to labour to put food on the table, 2. We are forced by law to pay taxes in order to dole out welfare, 3. We are forced to become bait for the same welfare recipient who, after spending his welfare money on tobacco, alcohol and drugs, decides to make himself worthy of, and deserving of free food in prison by taking a potshot at us, and 4. We still have to support him in prison, oftentimes in the style that we ourselves cannot afford.

It is conceivable that under the present food distribution system some people might go to jail to escape hunger and sleeping under the bridge. It is said that prison is not a nice place to be in. However, when it comes to survival, any place is better than laying in a gutter, with chattering teeth and a growling stomach. It is therefore possible that some minor crimes are committed to get some food and a place to stay, i.e. to get arrested. I have heard of one person who, during the Great Depression, as soon as the weather started to get colder, would break a window in the Court House and be incarcerated for the winter. After doing this for a few years he learned a trade of shoe repairing, while serving his sentence in jail, and from then on led a virtuous life. One may sometimes wonder if there is a significant difference between "freedom without money" and "money without freedom."

We should also keep in mind that being in jail is made disagreeable by the disagreeable people and not by the physical structure of the jail or its surrounding. Populate jails with those whom you consider to be nice, your mom and dad, your girlfriend, all of your best friends, and you would not wish for a better place to be in. With majority of people in jail it might even become dangerous to live out.

Free food staples would decrease the incidence of crime. It would make little sense for anyone to lose his freedom and be confined to small quarters, sharing a room with person one didn't like, wear striped prison uniform and eat inedible meals prepared by incompetent prison chefs.

Free food staples would reduce the incidence of drug addiction and alcoholism because no welfare money would support it, and it would be required that one be sober and drug-free for long enough to earn some money to spend on another bout of addiction. The enigma of alcoholism and drug abuse not being fully understood at the present time, only certain prediction could be made. If to drink makes a rational sense to the drinker, he would have less reason to drink under the free food staples plan.

For one thing, he would be able to achieve human dignity. Secondly, he would have no reason to hate his job, being free to quit it any time. Thirdly, he would not carry a heavy burden of responsibility to look after the sustenance of his family. Fourthly, he would not feel inferior being poor, since poverty would constitute a rational free choice available to everyone.

Free food staples plan would put the burden of responsibility for Substance Abuse squarely on the shoulders of the abuser. At this point many abusers are unable to afford the abused substance. They receive their help from social securities doled out to them in various forms. Thus, society supports their abuse. In addition, being able to receive the humanitarian aid of food from food banks, soup kitchens, churches and charitable organizations, and sleeping on the streets for shelter, all the money received from welfare could be spent on alcohol, tobacco and other abuse substances.

Ignorance of facts as they relate to drugs has nothing to do with the causes of addiction. Therefore, information and education is of no consequence here. Some well-informed and well-educated people from all walks of life smoke, drink and use recreational drugs. There is nothing that a student of social work can tell them that they don't already know.

The causes of drug addiction go deeper than that. They concern addicts' inability to make sense out of their lives without the use of alcohol, hallucinogenic and recreational drugs, in a society that is insensitive to their plight. The threat of shortening their lives by few months or years is not a deterrent. Meaningless and purposeless life is difficult to live even for a short while, so why would anyone want to prolong the agony?

A person has the inborn right to kill himself by any means to his disposal. He can do it by prescription drugs, alcohol, tobacco, cocaine and other addictive substances. He can do it by rope, knife or a gun. He can jump from high building or drown himself. Certainly, smoking marihuana will not do it for him.

The only way to prevent him from killing himself it is to keep him under constant surveillance in jail or institution. His violence towards himself makes sense to him and needs to make no sense to anyone else. He knows that his life is not livable in his hands and he tries to exit it with dignity. Keeping him alive against his will makes absolutely no sense to anyone. Torturing people by depriving them of all human dignity in jails creates jobs, but with the free food staples there would be no urgent need to be employed in this manner to put food on the table.

Government's active and forceful interference with the procurement of drugs by (perhaps) genetically challenged user, without creating a suitable environment for human dignity to shine forth, constitutes cruel and excessive punishment. Our social structure and the remedies provided to combat drug abuse and alcoholism may actually be the cause of it. We must therefore put our efforts and our money where our mouth is. We must create environment in which each of us would be free to fulfill his individual destiny and mission in life, and dignify ourselves in our own fashion. Let no one create for us jobs or provide us with "healthy" alternatives.

Let me again quote Pico dela Mirandola: "On man when he came into life, God the Father conferred the *seeds* of all kinds and the germs of every way of life. Whatever seeds each man cultivates will grow to maturity and bear in him their own fruit. If they were vegetative, he will be like a plant. If sensitive, he will become brutish. If rational, he will grow into a heavenly being. If intellectual, he will be an angel and the Son of God."

Legalization of addictive drugs made possible

Drug trafficking is obviously of no concern either to Canada or USA; otherwise these two countries would have done away with it at a drop of a hat. The most effective way to do it is by making drugs the monopoly of the state by underselling the competitor. Making all street drugs available in the pharmacies across the country at prices below those on the black market, quality controlled, available on prescription only, would ruin the black market drug trade. This can be realized by decriminalizing the drugs, which are now sold illegally on the streets. Failing this the drug traffickers will thrive. It is a job, it puts food on the table, business is good, and the risk of getting caught injured or killed is not greater than working in coalmines, flying a plane, driving a truck, or even fighting the drug trafficking itself.

Fighting drugs is a large industry, providing jobs for millions. One just has to add the number of all employees in drug enforcing agencies, the staffing of penal institutions guarding hundreds of thousands prisoners serving time on drug charges, the size of the judicial system, the legal profession, to arrive at the conclusion that with the present system of food distribution the opposition to legalization of street drugs could not be overcome. If putting food on the table is strong enough motivation to bring to extinction many of the endangered species, or deforest thousands years old rain forests, incarcerating each other serves the same purpose and is that much easier. It seems more preferable that one innocent person be arrested and fed in jail while feeding hundred others looking after him, than allow the guilty one to go free while feeding nobody. Arresting all smokers, drinkers, gluttons, body piercers, sex addicts, and lechers coveting their neighbours' wives, for their own good, could conceivably create 100% full employment and thus feed the entire country.

Free staples would open the door to the possibility of legalizing the now illicit drugs by destroying the monopoly of the black drug trade, by making it impossible to recruit the necessary prison guards amongst people who would be free to refuse to work, and by the lack of necessity of creating jobs.

Reverse discrimination against the working poor

In an article <u>Portrait of a panhandler</u> in the "Globe and Mail," Jan Wong described the life of a panhandler named Ms. Hallam. In principle, she led an ideal life. She was on welfare assistance and therefore did not have to work. However, she wanted to enjoy a few luxuries in life, for which welfare would not pay. They were a deluxe package of cable subscription, pack-a-day of cigarettes, occasional Mickey of rum, ability to pay the veterinary bills for her two "canine babies," and occasional eating in restaurants.

She knew that to be able to get these luxuries she had to take a personal responsibility and work to pay for them. And this is the way things ought to be in a just and rational society. She did not expect the taxpayer to foot the bill for these items, but went to work by collecting money for them in the same fashion as if she collected for the Heart & Stroke Foundation, or the Blind, albeit not being as open about it. She worked long hours, in rain and sunshine (without an umbrella), making $2-4 per hour, taking only Sundays off to rest up.

Mr Charbonneau of Jan Wong's article was in the same class as Ms. Hallam. He got from the government $515 each month, from which he paid $375 for a rooming house. This left him with $140 for food. If he wanted to smoke or watch cable TV he also would have to panhandle or perform small jobs. He was free to do it and he had plenty of time on hand to do it, but he decided against it.

While Ms Hallam enjoyed the privilege of choosing what to do to acquire the goodies, which made her life more meaningful, majority of working poor belonged to the underprivileged class, which was deprived of this freedom. Charbonneau's friend Pierre was fully employed, earning $6 per hour and working 40 hours a week. His total income at the end of the month was $960. After deductions for employment insurance, pension and income taxes he was not better off financially than Mr. Charbonneau, even though he lived in the same rooming house. However, there was this big difference between them: if he wanted to smoke or watch TV he would have to have another job, but he was too exhausted after work and did not have enough time to look for one. Pierre, therefore, was doomed to live without smoking or watching TV for the rest of his working days or else quit his job. Contrary to common wisdom, it would appear that only beggars on public assistance and pensioners could be choosers, whereas most working and taxpaying members of the society could not enjoy similar luxury.

These two examples point to the existence of the reverse discrimination against the working poor. Miss Hallam was living with one foot in the land of the free shelter and free food staples of tomorrow. She led a dignified existence in that she was free to panhandle or not to panhandle. Pierre, on the other hand, was pigeonholed on his job, which left him with no time and energy to lead a dignified life.

There are a number of things wrong with the above system: Miss Hallam had no option of choosing any other type of remunerative occupation beside panhandling without losing her status as a welfare recipient, and Pierre, although having the freedom to choose other jobs, had no time to do it. Also Miss Hallam was obtaining her alms under false pretenses, and was not paying food premiums or income taxes. What united them was their anxiety of not being able to put food on the table after losing their status of welfare recipient and fulltime worker.

Under the system of constitutionally guaranteed food staples, their anxiety concerning their future survival would be eliminated and both would have the dignity of choosing what they wanted to do with their lives. Miss Hallam, of course would have to pay $400 in food premiums, because panhandling at an average of $3 per hour, 4 hours a day, 6 days a week would put some $3,000 per annum in her pocket, $2,000 of which would qualify for a deduction of $400 for free staples food premium.

Diminished stress from the threat to survival

There is nothing more stressful in life than the threat to one's own and one's family survival. The insecurity of not knowing from where the next meal will come leads to stress-related disorders and anxiety. While contemplating one's own possibility of being reduced to the level of a homeless street beggar, of losing his job, home and health, one develops a tendency to horde goods, become niggardly and insurance-poor. Fear of losing poorly paid and mindless job on hand restrains one from looking for greener pastures and leads to overall dissatisfaction with life and proclivity to absenteeism from work because of various ills.

Morbid hording and saving diminished

Our self-preservation instinct makes us take measures to survive in the future, to hang on to our jobs, to save, to create one's own safety net. One is constantly harangued by prophecies of gloom and doom and there is no straw in sight to grab onto. The prices, the interest rates, the value of a dollar are in a constant flux. However, we know instinctively that if all the world goes to hell, if all industries close down, and all money becomes devalued to a zero point, if we become bankrupt, have no job, lose our homes etc., that if our food supply is secure, and if our health and mind is sound, we have nothing to worry about.

Our anxiety about the future makes us save disproportionately large amounts of money and deprives us of means to grow, to prepare ourselves psychologically for retirement, to acquire goods necessary for our individual pursuit of happiness, to learn, to gather experience, to travel etc. Banks seem to thrive on our anxieties but we suffer. Then, when the retirement age comes, we are physically and mentally incapable to do any of those things except to sit in a rocking chair and lovingly leaf through the pages of our bank saving books. The feeling of security under the free staples would permit the person to spend all his income now without having to save for pensions in his later years. This would constitute an added stimulus to the economy.

Absence of workfare

Under the free food staples plan _workfare_ would make no sense. No one would be degraded by being mandated to pick oakum or crush up stones to become deserving of life support. There, the right to life would be conferred on one by the fact of being born. No one else would have the right to deny him this right and force him to feel, to act, or to behave in any specific manner. The three-toed sloth would have as much right to life as cheetah. By the same token slothfulness and industriousness would have their place in the universal scheme of things. No one has enough knowledge or power of clairvoyance to declare any style of life as being politically incorrect, wasteful, useless, and without any merit.

Minimum wages eliminated

Minimum wage is the lowest amount of money, mandated by the government, to be paid to employed persons. It is ideological and leaning strongly towards dictatorship (see the mixture of magenta and yellow colours as a paradigm for capitalism). In other words the idea is capitalist but with strong socialist coloration in that it requires the free enterprise to assists government in its responsibility to feed people, while at the same time undermining the efficiency of the private enterprise to produce goods and services at competitive prices.

Since governments know of no other way to feed people, the question of subsistence is tightly woven into wages. They have to be made adequate to fulfill the workers' needs. Based on a normal working week of forty hours, the hourly pay has to be adequate enough to pay for one's food with some added monetary incentive to go on working. Minimum wages prevent some enterprises to stay in business since the sale of goods they produce, does not cover the expenses of producing them.

The free staples would make minimum wages meaningless and superfluous. They would therefore be eliminated. The rationale for this would be the fact that a person who is biologically able to survive, without being forced to take on a job, would be free not to work, or to work for any wages, or no wages at all, depending on his own good will, and the ability of his employer to pay him.

Labour unions and strikes eliminated

The function of Labour Unions is to protect interest of its workers, to prevent their undue exploitation by the company they work for, to increase the safety of the work place, to negotiate wages and fringe benefits, to mention just a few. These issues are important when a person is forced by an ideology to work under conditions for which he is not responsible, and so to say, put his life, health and his future on the line, in order to survive.

The equality of pay is another socialist term valid only in the circumstances in which a person is exploited while virtually fighting for his survival. He needs a strong Union to negotiate his wages, and a strong government overseeing the enforcement of the agreement. Availability of free food staples would make the existence of Labour Unions obsolete.

Elimination of workmen's compensation claims

A risk contained in any enterprise is a risk to one's life, health, and limb. To live means to be exposed to danger. One can never be sure what catastrophe will hit one, whether the earth will quake, tornado rip off the roof from his house, an object fall on his head from the sky, cancer or infection strike, or a person next to him go berserk. How then can another person or organization be made a scapegoat for our brand of misfortunes? However, when we exploit the need of our fellow men to survive and force them into a situation, which we known could be dangerous to them, then we do carry a responsibility for their welfare.

With free food staples guaranteed, everyone becomes an entrepreneur, exercising his freedom to take on any risks necessary for the success of his venture. The responsibility for his health and safety is his alone. It is like walking the tightrope over Niagara Falls, sailing around the world, climbing Mount Everest, diving to the bottom of the sea or volunteering to serve in the army. Governments and taxpayers should not be made responsible for the loss of life or limb in those ventures, because they are undertaken at the whim of the 'daredevils,' which term ideally ought to embrace all of us. However, when these projects are undertaken involuntarily, as is the case of being drafted into the army under the penalty of death or to obtain food to survive, the responsibility for their outcome rests with the political system (i.e. government and the labour unions), which sanctions the compulsion to participate. It must then vouchsafe the integrity of life and limb and establish a system of compensation.

As of now, government, although paying the lip service to the free enterprise, penalizes it by imposing on it an obligation to take financial care of its employees and their dependants in case of an accident. If it were not able to meet such obligation it would have to get out of business, although it would be perfectly viable without it. Free staples would reduce the costs of productivity by eliminating workmen's compensation.

Elimination of the sickness pay

A person who participates in a production or services of his own free will, without the pressure to make living, gets paid for his performance the agreed sum of money. He works to get profit on his investment of effort, but does not profit when he is sick. This is an orthodox business practice, without socialist expectation of getting something for nothing. The free staples would take care of his nourishment needs, and the National Health Plan would take care of his sickness. Why then would a sick person be rewarded for being sick?

Layoffs eliminated

Layoff under the present system of food distribution has an ominous and sinister ring to it. It means that a company has no more work for its workers and that as the result of unemployment they will have no income and in a long term nothing to eat. The concept of layoffs would become meaningless under the free staples plan. Its alternative meaning would be tantamount to interruption of the ongoing project for various periods of time: for a few days, for a weekend, for a season, for a year, etc. and for variety of reasons. Such interruptions would not make people unemployed, as this concept also would have no meaning.

Taking responsibility for one's life

Under the present food distribution system, we have created for everyone the world of utopia in which we as society teach and encourage irresponsible behaviour. Take for an example smoking and drinking. The taxpayer gives the welfare recipient money with full awareness that, if he is a smoker and a drinker, he will spent his welfare check on alcohol and tobacco. We know, and he knows, that if he ends up penniless the next day that we, the taxpayers, will feed him either in hospital, or in jail, or through food banks. If he develops throat cancer, he knows that we cannot refuse him medical help and he may even use our tax money to sue the doctor and the hospital for incompetent or negligent service. Thus we assist him in being irresponsible, in developing throat cancer in the first place and then, again at taxpayer's expense, with the help of the plastic surgeons, we assist him in reconstituting his face. Who profited from this experience? Who is irresponsible?

Free food staples would render such behaviour to be physically impossible. A smoker for example would not be able to smoke unless he earned enough money to buy himself a package of cigarettes. He could not sell the free food staples because they would have no commercial value in that everyone could pick them up at the store without running the risk of contamination and food tempering. There would be no welfare money doled out to him. Thus, he would have to knock on people's doors and ask if there was something he could do to earn $10 for a package of cigarettes.

Thus free food staples would permit a person to develop personal responsibility. He would take responsibility for his own life and contribute materially and spiritually to society. It would be impossible for him to act irresponsibly and this is good enough for me. I am not going to pick his brains to find if the lesson in taking responsibility was integrated.

This means that if he takes the responsibility to work to get money to buy for himself alcohol and tobacco, he is a responsible person, even if he happens to be a drug addict. I am not going to pay for a bartender to titrate his alcoholic intake. He is a free and responsible person who makes sense out of his life in his individually peculiar nonsensical manner. He knows that it is legal to kill oneself and that the law does not spell out that it must be done momentarily. So it will take him 40 years to die, so what? As George Burns the comedian said, his teetotaler doctor might be six feet underground while his chronically inebriated patient might still be struggling to accomplish the same by ever-heavier drinking bouts, but always responsibly, through his own effort.

Reforms of the present welfare system

Throughout the history, the present food distribution system served well all those who had money, derived chiefly from employment, business transaction and other legitimate and illegitimate occupations. It is the unemployed and moneyless with whom every society had difficulty to cope.

When we talk about welfare reforms or breaking the dependency cycle of the poor, we are talking about removing the hurdles, impediments, hostility, and discrimination that the society puts in the way of the poor to obtain their daily food sustenance. We are not conditioning people to live without food or altering their basic metabolism.

Under present food distribution system, the welfare recipient may have more cash in his pocket than the wage earner. This is most unfair and demoralizing to the worshipper of the work ethic. This creates two classes of people, those who work and for whom there are no free lunches, and those who deserve such free lunches by virtue of doing nothing.

It would seem to be logical to state that when a person says that he is disabled then he is truly a disabled person, for who is there to know better than himself? However this is not to be. Even to receive welfare one is put through the wringer. Giving of welfare is very complicated, very expensive business, which in the end does not address the real needs of the recipients. The taxpayer also resents it. He pays for the medical doctor, the psychiatrist, the psychologist, social worker, welfare worker, and all the minor and major bureaucrats, to examine the supplicant whether he is able to hold a job, and to ask him to prove that he is sincerely looking for one. He may have to submit every month a list of 30 prospective employers with their signature that 'yes, he was looking for a job, and no, there was no opening.' It is a humiliating process, as when a well-paid and inexperienced social worker notices a golden ring on the supplicant's finger and arrogantly suggests that 'if he was really that hungry he could have sold it.'

However, he who pays the piper calls the tune. At the present time one cannot get a free meal unless one proves to the donor that he is unable to pay for one. He has to be tested. A means test, eligibility test, aptitude test, or any test in general is a bad test if in the end it is non-discriminatory. If everybody passes it, or nobody passes it, then it is meaningless.

There is no eligibility test qualifying one to eat and stay alive. A means test or assessment of physical or mental disability, which would prevent one from seeking gainful employment, is superfluous, if in the end everyone is given a free access to food. Why then do we have welfare offices and pensions boards, and why do we file insurance claims, certifications of disability, if in the end it means one and the same thing: a person has to eat in order to stay alive, unconditional of his health, employability, willingness to work and financial status. A large bureaucracy assembled around this subject is too expensive to maintain. Its only purpose, as I see it, is to humiliate a fellow human being and to try to reform his nature by making him feel guilty for staying alive without giving to society anything in return.

Thus we do not starve to death an able-bodied person who applies for welfare while refusing to take on a job. Instead we appoint for him a spokesperson, usually a psychiatrist or a psychologist, who negates the meaning of his spoken words by branding him as not being in his right mind. Thus, having paid this price of being psychologically emasculated, he is permitted to eat without having to work. If such a practice is not dictatorial and based on some weird ideology, then which one is? A person who has lived together with himself since the time of his birth is the only one who knows intimately everything that there is to know about himself. When he says that he is unable to work then he is disabled. Which spokesperson in the world has the right and the knowledge to look him straight in the eyes and say: 'You are lying! *I know* that you are able.'

Free food staples would eliminate the welfare assistance, as we know it. It would enable the government to dismantle all presently existing social programs and use the money to repay the national debt. To be in possession of unearned sum of money would make a person a suspect of some shady, if not actually criminal activity. Situation would be similar to finding a $50 bill in the pocket of 8 years old boy. He could not have earned it by working, he could not have found it on the street, and a dirty old man giving it to him could not have exercised such a poor judgment in doing so. Ergo, how did he get it?

Doing away with beggars and panhandlers

No one could successfully panhandle for personal cause unless it was for humanitarian aid. Panhandlers, not unlike brand-name advertisers, tell the best story they can to make money. They appeal to the sentiment of the passers-by to spare a diem 'for something to eat and a place to stay.' Canvassing from house-to-house for a charitable cause is also a form of panhandling, exemplified by Salvation Army's Santa Claus, Scouts panhandling apples, Girl Guides selling chocolate bars and War Veterans red poppies.

Behind each of the panhandler's slogans there is implied plea for humanitarian aid, some of which is fraudulent. "I've just arrived from Bosnia" is as good a slogan as "I've just arrived from Albania or Burundi."

Panhandler knows quite well that were he to be honest and were he to ask the passers-by for a contribution to his deluxe cable package, a bottle of rum, cigarettes, crack-cocaine or to help to defray the veterinary costs for his dogs, he would not get very far. Hence a fraudulent plea: "Please spare any change for something to eat and a place to stay." Prepaid food and shelter plans would definitely expose such frauds.

One anecdotal story tells of a seemingly paralyzed beggar replying to a passer-by, commiserating with him over his paralysis: "Sir, nothing beats being paralyzed. Last month when I was blind I almost starved to death because people were throwing slugs into my hat."

Under the present welfare system there is no way of knowing whether the person begging is really hungry, either because he did not qualify for welfare, or the amount of welfare received by him was too small, or it was stolen from him, or he mismanaged it, or spent it on some addicting substances. One would have to be a hardened, dyed-in-the-wool neo-con, riding high on a horse of the work ethic, to refuse such request. The free food staples would remove the horse from under the neo-cons and convert them into ordinary pedestrians, also qualifying for free food and shelter, without being forced to take responsibility for their own lives by doing a dirty job, "just because somebody has to do it."

Thus the free staples would ease the conscience of the charity giver refusing to help on grounds that the beggar is not hungry. Guilt arises when we do not live up to the idealistic image of ourselves. We can bypass a panhandler on the street and tell ourselves that he is nothing but a businessman trying to make profit by panhandling, a Cadillac king or queen. However, now and then, we are beset by doubts. Perhaps he was really disabled, penniless and hungry, and we treated him in a callous fashion. With unobstructed access to the free food staples, not giving a penny to a beggar would not cause one to suffer pangs of bad conscience, since by not giving him anything one would only send him a message that there is no money to be had in panhandling.

Strengthening of the family ties

Free food staples would strengthen the family ties. Both parents would not have to go to work to make the ends meet. Children would not have to be put in foster homes or out for adoption, because of their physical neglect by their parents.

Reduction in the incidence of teenage pregnancies

Teenage girls wanting to lead an independent style of life and having difficulty finding a suitable job, or who are too young to qualify for work, sometimes get pregnant as a means to obtain welfare and mother's allowance. Thus, welfare psychology is being propagated from one generation to the next.

This sentiment was clearly enunciated by Gary Porter, Chairman of North Dakota Republican Party: "If a childless teenage girl applies for welfare, she is not eligible. But if she has a child, she is entitled to benefits worth at least $16,000 to $18,000 per year. That looks pretty appealing to a teenager wanting to get away from her parents."

In a sense, this teenager works by going through pregnancy and introducing to society a new member. She is rewarded with food for raising a future worker, soldier, welfare receiver, job creator or job provider. Living in poverty, her child will probably not get adequate education and will probably have to content itself with sawing on garment labels, working for some manufacturing company in her basement at home, and receiving below minimum wages.

With the availability of the free staples, doling out welfare would not be an option and getting pregnant would not bestow on the teenager any advantage. If anything, pregnancy would be more hindrance than help towards independence. The free access to food staples would in itself make her independent and provide her with incentive to finish school, whether living at home or away from home. Thus, to a degree that this is true, there would be a significant decrease in the rate of out-of-wedlock births.

Making spouses independent from each other

The free staples would free the spouses from their dependence on each other. A number of marriages have been contracted in the past for the sake of convenience. Some of them are held together by economic necessity. A woman who had multiple pregnancies and carried the entire responsibility for the household was in no position to look for a job and become independent. With the access to free food staples putting food on the table would not constitute an obstacle to a wife striking on her own. This option being realistic for her, her husband would treat her with more respect and the frequency of wife battering would decrease.

No need of food banks and soup kitchens

Soup kitchens and food banks would have no rationale for their existence with the availability of the free food staples. With grocery stores, supermarkets and milk bars open 24 hours a day, food staples would be available to anyone unconditionally and without bureaucratic encumbrance. They would be located close to the consumer. Every milk bar, small and large grocery store would effectively perform the function presently performed by the food banks.

Impossibility of going bankrupt

Any private enterprise in the present circumstances is a gamble, as large amounts of money need to be laid out with a hope of making a profit. If the demands of the market are miscalculated or rising inflation, interest rates and falling prices on the stock market make expenses exceed those of income, the entrepreneur is forced into the state of bankruptcy. In the end the taxpayer is the main loser.

Under the free staples there would be only an initial outlay of effort and not of capital. In the end if no profits materialized, the effort would have been wasted, love's labour would be lost, but no bankruptcy would follow. It would duplicate the patterns of games people play: a lot of energy is spent on e.g. wrestling, running or hitting a ball, with nothing to show in the end, and only pleasant memories remaining.

Inflation brought to a halt

For inflation to take hold there has to be general consensus amongst people to inflate. There has to be tightly organized business community, labour unions, governmental controls, plenty of legislation to enforce labour laws which govern hiring practices, set minimum wages, set interest rates, etc. There has to be a market value for everything. In other words, the situation has to be identical to the one existing at the present time.

General increase in prices of goods and services in a country is caused by escalating demands for higher wages and higher profits. It is a vicious spiral of murky origin, in which each person, small and large business, justify their claim of diminishing profits rising prices on grounds that they have to keep up with inflation. In turn, the demand for higher wages is blamed for increase in inflationary pressure. Labour, having to spend ever-higher portion of their income on food in proportion to other consumer goods, has no other choice but to go on strike.

Under the free staples the market would determine the cost of goods and services at the time of their sale and not in the beginning of the initiative or in the beginning of the manufacturing process. With retroactive pay, no minimum wages, governments staying out of enforcing the labour laws, and the labour force consisting of those who did not have to work, no goods and services would have an intrinsic financial market value. In such circumstances no individual would be in power to create inflation even if he badly wanted it. Thus, inflation as we know it would become obsolete, an archaic term under the plan.

Absence of politically correct or incorrect ideas

What is politically correct idea? It is an idea supporting the present system of work ethic in order to legitimize certain activity as work, and to criminalize others, which a person could justify as necessary for him to make living, such as hunting the endangered species, dealing in human organs, pimping, prostitution, surrogate motherhood, pornographic writing, criminal abortion, stealing, drug trafficking, etc. Politically corrected thinking is required to limit the evil imposed on us by work ethic, which says that 'job is necessary to make living and that you get paid for an honest day's work, that job is a job, and no work is undignified, etc.' Thus, politically correct idea is the whitewash on the work ethic. With the free staples there would be nothing that one could call politically correct or incorrect, since all activities would be the result of undertakings in accordance with one's free will.

Job creation unnecessary

Job creation is a misnomer and refers to the creation of an excuse by which a person gets paid. Thus, the fact of getting paid converts the recipient of the pay into a worker. His work may actually consist of not working, but just sitting or standing around, or holding an office, or being on call. It is make-work program, designed to keep him busy and thus deserving to be paid and staying alive.

Such an excuse is necessary under our present system in order to avoid giving an impression of free (unearned) handouts, which usually undermine the work ethic. However, to supply everyone with jobs, just so that they would be qualified to receive nourishment is too expensive proposition and beyond the powers of any governing body. Government creating jobs leads to a dictatorship and bloated bureaucracy.

The availability of free food staples would free the government from job creation and allow it to concentrate on the repayment of the national debt and organizing previously described activities. Job creation would lose its urgent appeal since everyone would be well fed, healthy and happy. Creation of goods and services would take precedent over job creation.

Increased competitiveness on foreign markets

Free food staples would offer an unprecedented competitive advantage on the world markets since everything for sale could be produced, in theory, without any costs at all, and undersold at any price. For how would one price the cost of a car, which was manufactured by workers who invested only their labour and might or might not be paid an indeterminate amount of money retroactively, only after the car was sold?

In reality it is only human labour and human willingness to cooperate that costs money but everything else in the nature is free. The sun and the moon, waterfalls, rivers, winds, oilfields, mines, etc, demand no payment. Given a guaranteed subsistence, shelter, health, and the good will, it would be theoretically conceivable to produce everything without even one penny of expenditure.

Only such a plan as this can create ideal conditions at home, for which the private enterprise is constantly on the lookout in faraway places: no labour unions, no strikes, no minimum wages, no affirmative action, absolute disregard of personal safety at the workplace, no pensions, health benefits, sick leave, family leave, maternity leave, workmen's compensation, etc., not even giving the workers money for food. Such conditions could not be found anywhere in the world at the present time, and without the free staples it never could exist. Even if a private company found a place somewhere in Africa or Asia, where workers would be willing to work for no pay, the cost of feeding them would outweigh the advantages gained.

Retirement pension is a soap bubble, which is liable to burst any time. It offers only a token of security for the future. The pot in which the money is kept has numerous leaks: inflation, taxation, currency devaluation, volatile interest rates, claw-backs, using pension funds to repay national debt, stock market speculation, embezzlement and fraud. When the time comes to collect, the money might have vanished or be there in piddling amounts.

It is not the money that we want when we retire but the guarantee that we will have enough food to subsist on. Give a starving person a fixed amount of money but nothing else, and it will take him a bit longer before he starves to death; don't give him a penny but feed him and he will live out his natural span of life.

Of course, one would always be free to save, to collect and to accumulate, not for rainy days but for the possibility of having the freedom to acquire goods produced by other people when and if one becomes so inclined. Under this plan the "fat pensions of the Boomers" would no longer exist. There would be no need for publicly sponsored pension plans since the free food would take care of the most important people's need. For the rest they would have to rely on their own private savings. Free staples would guarantee our survival at any stage of our lives, which a specified amount of money, doled out to a person in monthly installments would never be able to accomplish.

Reduction of budgetary deficit and debt repayment

Free food staples would help to reduce the Budgetary Deficit and the National Debt. Politicians aren't so much cutting social outlays as reallocating them. Social spending is flattening out rather than falling and is likely to remain steady, at least until the next recession. Five years ago Canadian government was on track to spend $97.7-billion on social programs.

I took the liberty to streamline (or to do away with) our social safety net, using grade 3 maths, and to show how much less complicated everything would be, if food staples were free. My calculations were based on the following assumptions:

1. There were 30 million people living in Canada
2. 16 million Canadians were remuneratively employed
3. 4 million were unemployed (i.e. receiving employment insurance)
4. There were 5 million Canadians over 65 years of age
5. 4 million Canadians were on welfare
6. 36,000 inmates were in federal and provincial custody
7. Proposed food premium, payable to the central collecting agency equaled $2,500/yr
8. Food premiums were payable on a sliding scale as follows: no payment on first $1,000, $100 on next $1,000, then 30% on the next $8,000, not exceeding the maximum of $2,500 on an income of $10,000/yr.

Based on the above premises, the total cost for the free staples plan would amount to $75 billion a year ($50/wk for each of 30 million Canadians). Everyone paid! There were no free lunches! The following were the sources of funding:

16 million of *employed* Canadians paid a total of $40 billions of food premiums for themselves (assuming that each of them earned a minimum of $10,000/yr). Assuming further that one half of them, i.e.8 million, earned a minimum of $20,000/yr, and *supported one dependent* (a spouse or a child), they would have paid an additional $20 billion for that one dependent. Four million of unemployed would have paid (would have their unemployment cheques reduced by the amount of food premium) $10 billion.

Fifty percent of the unemployed, 2 million supporting one dependent, would pay an additional $5 billion taken from their employment insurance cheques. The total of the above would have come to $75 billion, the estimated cost of the entire free food staples plan. More money would be coming from the following groups of people already receiving money from the social programs:

5 million SENIORS, receiving Old Age Security + Guaranteed Income Supplement, or CPP, would contribute (would have their cheques reduced by) $12.5 billion. 4 million of WELFARE recipients, whose income did not exceed $6,000/yr, would contribute $5.2 billion. All told, governments would end up with $17.7 billion of surplus money and could use the entire $97.7 billion budgeted for social programs on reducing their yearly budgetary deficits and the national debt.

New technology for doing dirty jobs

With newly gained freedom not to work one would not be able to push the hungry to do "a dirty job" because "someone has to do it." Invention and development of new technologies to dispose of garbage, to wash and clean, to go down into mines, to perform jobs dangerous to one's health and life would have to be made.

Disincentive to leave one's country

In one forum a story was told of two young men, James and his brother, finding it necessary to leave Canada because the country could not use them to make them feel _useful_. Also, a young lady with B.Sc. degree was made to feel useful and productive as a waitress in a coffee shop in Great Britain. Presumably she was unable to find appropriate job, which could utilize her skills in her own country.

How much of this is was due to the necessity of "finding a job to put food on the table?" Under circumstances, as they existed in Canada then, only Uncle Sam was smart enough to capitalize on their "world class education" and without "worrying about a language or culture barrier" he was willing to use them, pay them appropriate usage fee, and thus make them feel useful and productive members of society.

Food staples being freely accessible, there would be no pressing need for anyone to seek employment offshores. James and his brother, therefore, together with the prospective waitress with B.Sc. degree, would take their time to find out what would fulfill them in their lives, what was their purpose of living, and what was their mission and goal in life. The free food staples plan would give all new graduates with post-secondary certificates an incentive to stay in the country of their birth, and enable every individual to find and define the parameters of their own usefulness.

In their own soul-searching they would evaluate their inborn talents, the strength and weaknesses of their personality, their interests and their long-nurtured dreams. Other people wanting to use them for their purposes would be irrelevant to their own ideas of how they would be willing to let themselves be used.

After this self-evaluation James and his brother could hypothetically come to a conclusion that Uncle Sam wanted to use them for purposes foreign to their own lifelong aspirations, which might have been: observing the celestial panorama, searching the skies for comets and meteoroids and developing means to get in touch with other civilizations in the universe. Uncle Sam said that there was no money in it. He described to them how he would use them, i.e.: to develop market strategies, to detail the specific product to the prospective customers, to follow market trends and to balance the books. This usage of them, however, was not guaranteed for longer than the length of their one-year contract, following which they would have to search for a new user. In spite of the warmer climate, they conceivably would decline Uncle Sam's invitation, take control of their lives and go back to school. The morale of their reflection would have been something like this: To be useful one had to use oneself in fulfilling one's mission in life and perchance find a patron who would pay him for doing just that.

The prospective waitress, under the system of free food staples, could have decided to become an amateur stage actress, the dream she might have had as far back as she could remember. She might have arrived at the insight that to be used as a waitress in a coffee shop did not really made her feel very useful, in spite of substantial user fee, topped by even higher tips from the customers. Because there was no money in acting she was forced to wait on customers in order to put food on the table. Now she would be able to be an actress because the free staples guaranteed her survival. She would perhaps be paid retroactively, variable amounts of money, depending on the sales of the tickets, but this would be acceptable to her.

Love your neighbour as yoursef coming to fruition

The free staples would bring to fruition 2,000 years old Christian ideal "Love your neighbour as you love yourself," which preachers, missionaries, crusaders and inquisitors had failed to make stick. It would make people more tolerant of each other (more Christian?). As things stand now, loving one's neighbour is outright dangerous. In a society founded on principles of workfare, where everyone is primarily foraging for food, one has to growl in a doglike fashion each time someone comes too close, while one is gnawing on a mutton bone. In these jungle-like conditions, every person wears a civilizing disguise, hiding an animal within. By the time one finds out that the 'lovable' neighbour was a fox, a vulture, or a lion in the sheep's clothing, it is usually too late. Most of our literary works abound with the themes of this kind.

In the real jungle conditions are more honest and straightforward. One knows who is who by the scent of his body, kilometers away. The instinctual knowledge guards zebra from preaching brotherly love to a lion. The one, which does not know any better, is not fit to survive. Free food staples would permit everyone to lower his guards, because no one would have the need, or power to deprive him of his livelihood.

No need for affirmative action

Affirmative action under the present system serves to provide equal employment opportunity and prevents discrimination in admission, hiring and promotion practices in the working place, based on race, colour, religion, gender, sexual preferences, or national origin. Some consider it a milestone and others as a remedy for intractable social disease. To my way of thinking it as a disease.

Affirmative action is a band-aid treatment of a disease caused by a government, using its dictatorial powers to impose on its subjects the idea that in order to eat everyone must provide justification by having worked for it. It is a form of social engineering the purpose of which is to even the playing field and to facilitate the access to the trough for everyone.

Free staples would permit the free enterprise to get rid of this millstone around its neck. As an entrepreneur why would he be mandated to use the reverse discrimination and hire a person unsuitable for the job just because he/she is a woman, black, disabled, or whatever? It is obviously necessary under the present circumstances, but most burdensome and shackling to the enterprise, depriving it of its freedom to produce goods and services at competitive prices. Such practices would be unjustified with the availability of the free staples. Only those enterprises, which discriminated the most in favour of efficiency, quality, and cost effectiveness, would have the best chances to survive.

Increased socializing between people

Food is an important ingredient in any social functions. It is hard to imagine a get-together between friends and relatives, a meeting or a convention in which full course meals, drinks or cookies would not be served. Notwithstanding other causes for the lack of socializing between people, the lack of staples contributes heavily towards that end. One could safely say that struggling for the resources necessary to maintaining one's household and thus not finding enough food to entertain friends and relatives is a major alienating factor amongst the people. Free food staples would remedy this deficiency.

Population explosion and size of family halted

Children contribute to household expenses when they are old enough to work. This is one of the reasons that families have many children in some countries. It is a form of "social safety net." Thus if some of the "adults" are out of work, there are others to ensure that everyone stays nominally fed, clothed and sheltered. Free food staples would slow down the need for large family by providing such social safety net.

'Deficit' and 'economy' obsolete terms

Having ironclad, constitutionally guaranteed right to food, such terms as 'deficit,' 'economy,' 'stock market,' would become irrelevant to individuals not involved in the business of monetary transactions. The premiums paid would cover the expenses of the staples on the menu. One could not have what was not on the menu. If the price of the staples went up the amount of the premiums would also have to be increased. If there was a worldwide shortage of staples, they would have to be rationed. If the rations were too small, everyone would have to go hungry and slowly starve. In times of famine the fittest ones would survive. Food has to come first. Without it there would be no people and without people there would be no society, no stock markets and no economy.

With the availability of the free food staples the average consumer would not need to have his digestive processes disturbed by his worry of the system going broke, stock market collapsing, or unemployment rate going sky-high. The collection of premiums would lie with the administrators of the plan, the procurement of staples would be in the hands of many private enterprises with treasury department of the plan footing the bill.

NUTS AND BOLTS

FREE FOOD STAPLES PLAN IN GENERAL

The free food staples plan is not an ideology and not a program. It is simply a method of payment. One can pay or prepay, do it by writing a check, by credit card, by cash, by promissory note, etc. It is not any different from buying things on Visa and saying: "I will pay at the end of the month when the payment becomes due," or as in this case, pay by quarterly installments or by the end of the year; pay by premiums, taxes, or prices each time I make a purchase. All armies in the world, hospitals, institutions and jails function on this principle. Prepackaged travel tours have meals prepaid.

The key element in the Free (read prepaid) Food Staples Plan is its universality. When I pay food premium I do not provide benefits to anyone else but only to myself. It is like buying a package tour with all meals prepaid. There may be on that tour a dozen of travelers weighing 250 pounds each (twice as much as I weigh), who would outeat me anytime, but I would not stop to consider whether my money paid for their meals. Why would I be resentful that the "profit" or "surplus" from the food premiums would feed or house some sloth, if all I am doing is buying for myself the privilege to have a free access to the staples?

Under this system no staples could be sold to anyone, because no one would pay for something, which they could get free. Supposed one checked out 10 dozens of eggs and tried to sell them to his neighbour. Why would he risk contamination and pay for a product that might not be fresh, kept out of refrigeration for too long? He may be willing to pay for the convenience of not having to go to the store himself, a sort of delivery charge. But, this can be done even now.

Free staples plan would considerably simplify the food distribution and be more cost effective than it is now. The grocer's handling fees being constant, the day-to-day variation of market prices for each staple would be of no concern to the consumer. Thus saving would be derived from not having to ticket each staple item. In addition all financial transactions at all levels would be eliminated, making downsizing to the bear bones possible. The plan would also guard against wastage in that no handling fees could be charged to the single payer for the items that were spoiled and then discarded and therefore not taken out by the customer.

The money would change hands only at the highest level between the producer and the revenue department collecting food premiums. A private corporation would ideally run it. From there on, down the line, charges would be made to the single payer each time a value was added to the product.

The availability of free food staples would not violate anyone's right to eat anything and anywhere. Just the fact that e.g. a given bag of flour is free does not force anyone to limit his consumption to this kind of brand. Unlimited number of brands of the same flour would be available besides the prepaid one. They would carry different prices from the sublime to the ridiculous. There would be nothing to prevent a consumer to pay e.g. $10 for a bag of flour, containing an ingredient "X" rather than avail himself of the same one free of charge but not listing such an ingredient.

Any eating establishments would not need to reflect their lower costs because they used free staples. To make a profit in addition to their service and handling charge, they would be able to charge what the market could bear. There would be no price controls. However, the prepaid staples would permit them to stay in business longer before declaring bankruptcy. Cutting costs would be done not to benefit the consumer but to stay in business and make larger profit. If the market could not bear the cost of production of an item then the business would have to close. With availability of free food staples no good businessman would charge exorbitant prices for a meal, knowing that his prospective customer could grab a bun and a piece of cheese for nothing, just around the corner.

There would be no provider class, or for that matter no classes, either of homeless and hungry to be provided for, or of those doing the providing. The grocery employees would work for wages as they do now; the free food staples not requiring that the services to implement it should also be free.

THE MANNER OF FINANCING

The Free Food Staples Plan would be financed by monthly food premiums, which each member of a society, without exception, would be required to pay, depending on their yearly income or the income of their caregivers. In other words, it would be financed from the same sources that it is financed at the present time. The difference would lie in the streamlining and modernizing of the method of collecting the money which would save a good deal of effort, humiliation, inconvenience, irritation and finally the cost.

Presently, each time a person pays for his staples he has to count dollars and cents and the amount has to be entered into the cash register and the change handed out and counted, or else he has to write a cheque or amounts have to be entered on his credit card. All of this is accompanied by waiting, searching, counting etc. The panhandler has to get money by begging for something to eat on the streets. The charitable institutions, soup kitchens and food banks have to canvass for donations. The shoplifter has to be constantly monitored and if caught, charged, prosecuted and punished. The disabled has to undergo questioning, testing, assessment of his ability to work. The unemployed has to be prodded to seek employment. The welfare recipient has to be harnessed into the workfare. All of these procedures are costly, degrading and unnecessary, because in the end no one is allowed to starve to death.

The free food staples would by necessity allow anyone who had no money to pay no premium, without attempting to starve him into employment so that he would be able to pay. The initial estimation of the premium would be based on real numbers derived from Statistics Canada, as they concern the consumption of the staple foods in Canada, on spot-surveys and on calculation of prices of staple foods based on certain caloric and nutritional requirements. The fine-tuning of the amount of the food premiums, raising or lowering, would be accomplished at the end of each taxation year.

Everyone in our society who had an income would pay food premium. As an example one could choose an arbitrary figure of

$2,500, which the average Canadian spends on staples consumed by him each year. (This amount is more than twice of that which Mike Harris, Premier of Ontario, allowed the welfare recipient = $90/month X 12= $1,080).

A person earning less than $1,000 a year would pay nothing, but he would also receive no money. He and his dependents would be entitled to go to any grocery store and pick up any staple food free of charge, in unlimited amounts and without any bureaucratic tape. Food premiums would be payable on a sliding scale as follows: 10% or $100 on next $1,000, then 30% on the next $8,000, not exceeding the maximum of $2,500 on an income of $10,000/yr.

Present day welfare recipient with an income of $5,000 a year would pay $1,000 i.e. $83 a month. This would be deducted from his monthly welfare cheque. Old Age pensioners and Canada Pension recipients with an annual income of over $10,000 would pay full $2,500 in food premiums, i.e. $200 would be deducted each month from their pensions, and from their employment insurance, etc. In other words all forms of social assistance would be cut by the amount of food premiums. More would be cut with introduction of the shelter plan, until all monetary payments to the recipients could be eliminated.

Each dependent would be subject to the same premium rule. If his/her spouse and children made $1,000/yr or less a year, they would pay no premiums. If their income was $10,000 or more, they would pay only $2,500/yr. A spouse or a child old enough to pay income taxes would be treated as dependents or independents, depending on the choices made by their caregiver, or by the department of revenue.

Assuming that the person in question made $50,000/yr and listed his wife and five of his children, less than 16 years of age, as his dependents, none of whom earned an income, his yearly food premium would amount to $12,500 ($2,500 for himself and $10,000 for his wife and the three children). He would not pay any food premium on the remaining two children, unless his total income was $70,000/yr)

A person, or a family, out of the country for longer than 30 days would be entitled to claim the refund on their food premiums, upon presenting the evidence of such an absence, at the end of each taxation year.

A visitor entering the country would pay a food premium based on the length of his proposed stay in the country (as evidenced by his/her return flight ticket). A $50 per week would translate into $10 per day for a visitor, paid up front. Upon changing his status to that of landed immigrant, he would be treated as a dependent of the person who sponsored him. If later given a status of landed immigrant, he would be subjected to the same premium payments as the a full fledged citizen

THE NATURE OF STAPLES

Staples are that kind of food which form a basic part of our everyday diet: bread, flour, sugar, rice, pasta, eggs, butter, milk, cottage cheese, chicken meat, hamburger meat, cooking oils, potatoes, carrots, onions, cabbage etc. My definition would be: any natural product which could be eaten raw, or out of which a meal could be prepared by cooking, which product is necessary for survival and maintenance of good nutrition and good physical health. Medical doctors, nutritionists and dietitians would have a say in it. In the end, I believe, most foods could be on the list since eating habits of one would be balanced by those of another, according to the wisdom expressed in the Mother Goose Nursery Rhyme:

"Jack Sprat could eat no fat, His wife could eat no lean, And so betwixt them both, you see, they licked the platter clean."

Ultimately staples would constitute any foods that were put on the menu. What was not on the menu would have to be individually purchased. The preparation and delivery to one's door would not be a part of the plan. He who would not get it would have nothing to eat. It would be up to the individual.

Staples would be looked at as a public good, as if it were a variety of procedures under the country's universal health system, or a free access to the highways. The consumer himself would decide what staples he wanted, as he did when he went to a physician and chose which part of his body he wanted him to examine, to x-ray or to operate on, or which road to take and where to go.

The quality of the staples would not have to be inferior to those under the present system, as it would have to be, if it were a private enterprise geared on making profit. Thus bread, for example would not have to be stale or ground beef contain extra fat added to it. Since this plan is not operated for profit, nothing could be gained by such practices. The stale bread or stale supplies of other products would only cut into the grocer's amounts of handling fees and also force the consumer to patronize other grocery stores.

Staples would also not have to be, as one of the participants in the discussion group described, " seasonal, regulation Canada Food Guide fare, decided by experts, indifferently prepared, delivered hot/cold to one's door on a daily basis" They would neither be prepared, heated up, nor delivered to one's door on the daily basis.

Free food staples would not include readymade hamburgers, because the free staple of ground beef in the burger would contain an added value of labor involved in preparing hamburgers, maintaining the premises, and providing the service. However the price of burgers e.g. at McDonald's could be cheaper, made possible by the fact that McDonald's too would get their staple of ground beef free.

Strawberries, not being essential for living, would not be a benefit under the plan and therefore would call for out of pocket expenditure. However a number of fruits and vegetables homegrown and in season could be temporarily declared as staples. Chinese food, not being classed as staple food, would also not be free of charge, although some ingredients that went into preparing it might be. It would fall into the category of restaurant meals or ready-made food, TV dinners etc.

Under the Plan eating in restaurants would not be free, although meals could be cheaper since one would not pay for staples that went into their preparation. In restaurants one would pay for the use of premises, the ambiance, the labour of food preparation and the service.

STAFF AND DISTRIBUTION CENTERS

Everyone would shop in their habitual way going to their favorite grocery stores, as before. There would be no supervision of any transaction and no limitation or rationing of the staples. All moneychangers, starting with cashiers, accountants, bank clerks, bank managers to personnel working for the Ministry of Finance, would be considerably reduced in numbers. In the end the Plan would require no bureaucrats whatsoever.

There would be no reason to have separate food-staples-warehouses, or food depots, as every grocery store would carry them. Existing grocery stores and supermarkets run by private enterprise would be sufficient for the purpose. Also, there would be no reason to carry only the low quality staples. After all, everyone would consume these staples, without discrimination against the poor, homeless, and the hungry and without the discrimination against the wealthy or obscenely wealthy. The free food articles in a supermarket would be treated in the same fashion as any other articles in the store. The only noticeable difference would be reflected on the cash register slip, showing articles with no charge.

Under the plan, all staple foods would be carried on the shelves of all grocery stores, supermarkets, milk bars, convenience stores, etc. They would be packaged in distinct wrappers and carry a distinct logo and a bar code indicating that they were free of charge, similar to no-brand-name products. Consumer would make the choice on the retail level. Which items would be designated as being free of charge would have to be negotiated between the food producer (processor) and the business administration of the free food plan. It would follow the pattern set by the Ontario Drug Plan, as described below:

The fact that most seniors and welfare recipients in Canada obtain their drugs on a drug plan, free of charge, does not stop pharmaceutical companies from competing with each other. Generic drug companies sell the same-patented drug of the same quality at much lower price. Profits are the main motivating force behind any monetary transaction, whether the drug is paid for by the individual or by the drug plan. Government does not purchase any drugs. On advise of pharmacologists and doctors it approves payments for certain drugs and not for the others. Pharmaceutical companies negotiate the approval of payments for a given drug and, if there are no cheaper substitutes and the drug is essential for treatment of certain life threatening disorders, government agrees to put it on the drug plan. The pharmacies, however, carry all the drugs: those sold over the counter, on prescription, whether covered or not by the drug plan. Food would be handled in a similar manner. Inedible or indigestible food would be shunned by the consumer and eventually taken off the list of the foods approved for payment. Profits would be lost, and the quality would have to be improved.

The supermarkets would not only carry one brand of the free food staples, but also the competitive brands. Besides, they would carry the full range of products that were not free, as they do it at the present time. For an example, just because a bakery carried several varieties of the basic bread, recognizable by the distinctive prepaid-food-wrapper, it would not stop also carrying dozens of other varieties of bread, pastry, and cookies, for which one would have to pay. Just because the supermarket would carry the prepaid flour, sugar, cooking oil, potatoes, chicken, eggs, etc. would not necessitate it emptying its shelves of all the jams, cereals, delicatessen items, prepared foods, frozen pizzas, TV dinners, soft drinks, etc., etc.

The producers of the free staples would be in competition with each other and the consumer, as always, would have the final say. If supermarkets carried staples unsuitable for human consumption, they would lose their clientele and would not be paid their customary handling fees since the staples would not have gone through the checkout.

Competition between the products is only partially based on their quality and prices. Two bags of identical flour for instance, one with a prepaid food-logo and free of charge and the other, packed in different wrapper, with different picture, listing different contents, bearing a higher price, would have an equally competitive chance to be picked up by the consumer loaded with money.

Theoretically speaking, the number of possible brands of e.g. wheat flour could reach infinity. This could be accomplished by the producer listing what they do not contain and this could go into tens of thousands e.g.: "does not contain gluten, ergot, lead, arsenic, strychnine, cyanide, weevils, excrement of weevils, unsaturated fats, cholesterol, levulose, dextrose, fructose, pollens, fungus, yeast, etc., etc. Combine this with what it can contain, and how much of each, in fractions of a gram. Then add to it the variety of packaging and commercial art pictured on it, the place of its origin, the amounts contained in each package plus prices per gram and numerous fancy names, and the snob appeal becomes irresistible.

The grocer would be paid by the Plan a negotiated handling and storage fee for each staple, based on his customary average handling fees of the same and similar items for the past several years. Each staple would bear a bar code and would have to be checked out at the cashier's counter together with other chargeable articles. A software program would keep a record of handling fees and sum them up at the end of the day, e.g. 10 cents for each dozen of eggs taken out, 10 cents for each loaf of bread etc. At the end of the day the computer would send the bill electronically (without bureaucratic prompting) to e.g. <freefood@prepfood.ca> (Home page <http:// www. prepfood.ca>) and the money would be electronically deposited in the shopkeeper's bank account.

It would be up to the grocer to pay any helpers that he would employ, plus all the expenses connected with running of the grocery store, as he was wont to do in the past. It would be to his advantage to carry all prepaid food staples in his store in addition to all other grocery items and competitive chargeable and non-chargeable staples, which would enable the consumer to make his shopping in one place.

Everyone would shop for staples in the grocery stores as usual without any outward signs that anything had changed. The only difference would be noticed on their cash register slips in that there would be no charge for the designated staples. Also no one would be doling out these products nor would there be set rations. As to standing in line to 'receive rations' would depend on how many chargeable articles the shopper in front would have in his shopping cart to check out. Also, such archaic concepts as 'receive' and 'rations' would not apply here, since it would be the prepaid staples, which he would himself take from the shelf and bring to the checkout counter.

SHOPPING IN PRACTICE

This is what the shopping in the era of the free food staples would look like: We enter the SuperMart. The shelves are full of merchandise. There are dozens of brand name products of everything that we normally find in a Supermarket. We are looking for a bag of flour and find several brand names of 5 lbs. bags on the shelf: 'Monarch' at $4.00, 'Robin Hood' at $5.00, 'SuperMart Own Brand' at $2.00 (expressly milled by Robin Hood Foods Ltd. for this store), and lastly a 5 lb. bag of flour labeled: 'Prepaid Food Staples,' also milled by Robin Hood Foods Ltd., without any price tag.

I take the prepaid flour and a box of Kellogg's frosted cornflakes; you choose only a bag of 'Robin Hood' flour. We go through the checkout counter. My cash register slip shows $2.00 charge for cornflakes and no charge for flour. You pay $5.00 for your flour. What is wrong? You expressed your consumer's individuality by buying 'Robin Hood' brand. You did not pay $5.00 for flour because this staple was paid by you in advance by your food premium. So what did you pay for? For the label, for advertising, for special packaging, for some secret ingredient listed on the label, for sweet nothings assuring you invigorating feeling and good health, and most importantly for the opportunity to give you a choice. Thus freedom to assert your individuality was safeguarded.

There are no monitors in sight. There are no limits imposed on the amounts of food taken out, unless certain articles become momentarily in short supply, due to conditions beyond one's control, when only a specified number of articles would be allotted per person, until the supplies are replenished. In this respect things are as they always have been. Some people take more and eat more. The size of one's stomach and of one's appetite sets the limits and everyone is his own judge.

There are no vouchers, no Big Brother, no unwieldy bureaucracy, standing in lines, doling out stale bread and fatty cuts of beef, feeding the poor, etc. As a matter of fact the free staples have nothing to do with the poor, with the food stamps, food rationing, soup kitchens or food banks. It is a commercial transaction on the high level, a simplified direct method of providing staple food for all people, rich and poor, without relying on redistribution of taxes, the value of the dollar, food prices, interest rates or the rate of inflation and unemployment. It removes from the individual the unnecessary anxiety as to where his next meal is going to come from. It is prepaid by food premiums or taxes in the same manner as national defense, the salary of governmental bureaucrats, education, highways, health, fire insurance, life insurance, are prepaid.

No special cards to prove that the premium was in fact paid would be issued. Like taxes, the IRS would collect premiums for prepaid staples at source. Just as the cashier at the checkout counter would never ask any customers whether he paid his income tax, and did he have a card to prove it, he would not ask for the proof of the prepayment for staples.

MANNER OF IMPLEMENTATION

A referendum would need to be held after everyone in the country had an opportunity to read and digest the arguments made in this book in favour of a single payer; premium supported Free Food Staples Plan.

Once the decision is made to proceed, the implementation of the Plan would be instantaneous, i.e. it would take no longer than it takes to organize various departments, hire the necessary staff and publish the details. Conceivably the following instructions would be sent to all the taxpayers: "If your income in the last taxation year was $10,000 or more, your quarterly food premium remittance should equal $625. If your income was less than $1,000, disregard this letter. Please use enclosed Food Premium Tables for the incomes in between."

A letter to the employers would instruct them to add to the monthly income tax deduction an appropriate amount of the food premium. A letter sent to all grocery store owners would inform them that e.g. as of the first of the next month all the staples of the prepaid food items would bear appropriate bar-code, which would specify the handling fees for each, and how to get electronically paid. The payment would be automatic at the end of each business day. It would be against the law to charge the customer for the free staples.

A letter sent to all the pensioners, the receivers of Old Age Supplement, welfare, social assistance, etc., would inform them why their cheque was short by certain amount of money, reflecting their payment for food premiums and how much better off they will be in the future on account of the introduction of the Free Food Staples Plan.

The Plan would have to be universal and compulsory; otherwise it would be impossible to assure that non-participants to the plan would not take advantage of it without contributing financially towards its maintenance.

OTHER PREPAID ITEMS

It is the fact that man does not live by bread alone. He needs other things besides food. Amongst these are shelter, clothing, transportation, and health care. Oftentimes this hierarchy of human needs is used to deny people even their most basic needs i.e. arguing that "if you give people food, they will want shelter and clothing, and if you give them that they will want a car, therefore, the best policy is not to rock the boat by giving them any food, or even letting them breath!" With this caveat in mind my rephrased ultimate proposal would read: Universal Compulsory Free Food Staples, Health, Shelter, Education, Transportation and Clothing Plan.

These needs would have to be taken care of for people's optimum functioning. I define "a need" as "goods and services, the lack of which would result in poor physical and/or mental health or existential death of the individual." There is unbridgeable gap between biological and personal needs of an individual, each of which requires an outlay of variable sums of money. Because everyone needs to eat, everyone needs to have money in order to do so; therefore everyone needs to have a job. To have a job means that everyone has to perform some sort of action for which he gets paid. This need, to have three square meals a day, is persistent and continuous.

No one has to decide for one what is a want and what is a need. If one says that he had needed a motorcycle and this need was not fulfilled for the past year, then he knows that it could not have been a need that he had, or else he would have died a long time ago. On the other hand, if he says I want a warm jacket or something to eat and he does not get it for a day or two, his body lets him know that it is a need and not a want that he has.

Thus shelter, clothes and health services would be classed as a need. Surely we do not want to see people freezing on the streets with a dented can of tuna and a half-rotten baloney sandwich in their hands, because of such abstract notions as interest rates, inflation and high rate of unemployment.

There are no limits to man's desire. The hungry person desires foremost food, but after he had been sated he moves on to fulfill his other desires. Now, what happens when he just keeps on desiring but makes no effort to satisfy them? Nothing! Or the same as happens when he works for a company and goes on strike. What does the company do when he desires to drive Mercedes or Rolls Royce? Absolutely nothing! If anything, it may wonder about his sanity. If his demands are reasonable and his services are irreplaceable and the financial state of his company is healthy, he may get the assurance that the company may give the matters careful consideration and perhaps grant him a pay increase.

Shelter may appear to some to be a bigger problem for people than food. However, it may help us to remember that the kind of humanitarian aid, which we extend to people struck by natural disasters in any country of the world consists primarily of food and potable water. They all are in danger of primarily dying of starvation and not from overexposure to the elements, therefore we deliver to them food and clean drinking water first. The well-fed body provides enough heat to keep itself warm and another living body may provide sufficient shelter to prevent the heat loss even if no other physical objects were to be seen on the horizon.

The idea of a prepaid shelter occurred to me when, some years ago, my wife and I went to see an opera performance at the MET in New York. We inspected the rooms at the YMCA, located near Lincoln Center, but rejected them at $25 a night in favour of the nearby Imperial Hotel at $100 a night. Had the shelter at the YMCA been prepaid we still would have opted out for the more luxurious room at the Hotel. Things, of course, would be different if we had no money.

Concerning shelter provision, government would have to mandate that each hotel should have a percentage of rooms designated as shelters in the same fashion as service stations, restaurants and public buildings are mandated to have a certain number of washrooms. They would be rated as one quarter to one half stars, be accessible to anyone wanting to use them, without the proof of entitlement, and provide a minimum amount of service and comfort. The private owner of the hotel-shelter would periodically submit a bill to the shelter-paying agency for each day that the shelter was utilized.

With the prepaid food and shelter plan in place, one would move to tackle transportation. At first it would be from city to city, by railway, in boxcars, sitting on hard benches, very slow and inefficient and without the air-conditioning. As to the clothing, a government issue boots, basic jeans, and tops, similar to those clothing articles available through the army surplus stores, available to all who would not mind wearing them, just by asking, would be sufficient for the purpose.

This accomplished, the welfare society as we know it would be effectively eliminated and therefore not in need of reformation. No pocket money would be handed out to anyone as part of his or her entitlement. Thus for a trifle and without the pains of labour, we would have created a society free of welfare recipients, free of food-banks and soup kitchens, free of beggars, panhandlers and homeless, and free of the concepts of employment and unemployment.

FREE STAPLES IN OTHER COUNTRIES

Could this plan be introduced in any other country in the world? A country would first have to produce sufficient amounts of food to be independent of imports. Then, there would have to be well-developed transportation and delivery system and sufficient number of grocery stores and supermarkets. The GNP of a given country would have to be at least equal to the costs of the consumed staples.

Deserts have sand and a lot of renewable energy from the sun. The air there, as everywhere else, contains 78% of Nitrogen. They also have plenty of water if only the rainwater drainage could be stopped. Water in space station e.g. is being constantly recycled and reused. Not a drop of it is wasted. What is possible in a small area, with limited water supply, for the span of several months, should be possible over larger area of the desert, if all the water from rainfalls could be stopped from escaping. With all human and animal waste recycled and water conserved, and with the external financial assistance and the know-how of the affluent countries, enough food could be grown to enable the governments of the desert countries to supply its population with free food staples on prepaid basis.

The countries enjoying the free food staples system would have a luxury to sell their food surpluses to the needy countries of the world and to donate some of it as a humanitarian aid to those afflicted by natural disasters. The foreign aid would primarily be concerned with helping countries to become self-sufficient in food.

ABUSE AND WASTAGE IN THE SYSTEM

It is difficult to visualize scenarios in which food abuse and waste would endanger food supply and food consumption in the country. Because an individual does not deal with money, the potential for food abuse is negligible. One of the participants of the Free Staples Forum argued: "If I can get all the bread I want, why would I even bother to close the bag and try to keep it fresh? I'll just get another fresh loaf tomorrow when I want it!"

To throw away one-day-old bread is like losing a penny from a piggy bank. Also, it requires effort to do it. However, some waste, in everything we do, is unavoidable. Combustion engines lose a good deal of their energy in the form of heat, houses lose their heat through inadequate insulation, lights are left on in unoccupied rooms, people load their plates at smorgasbord dinners and leave most of food on them untouched.

Perhaps, because the food is so vital for our survival, the nature built into it safeguards against waste and abuse. For one thing, nature does not depend on legal, professional and moral qualities of people; if it did we probably would have been extinct by now. Food is perishable, bulky and too conspicuous, unlike money, which cries to be abused. This monetary plea for abuse is almost impossible to resist and the damage done by such an abuse may have worldwide repercussions. (Just witness organized crime controlling banking system in Russia). On the other hand, the size of one's stomach, the caloric requirements of one's body and the state of one's health put limits on the amount of food ingested. My desire for comfort and natural degree of inertia and slothfulness makes me close the paper bag and keep my bread fresh so that I would not have to go to the grocery store tomorrow. If I don't work, I have no car or gasoline, and I do not feel like walking, but if I work I am too exhausted to shop for groceries every day. Paying for an additional garbage bags exerts an additional deterrent on my wastefulness.

Scraping the barrel, one might think that perhaps the shopkeeper could abuse the plan by submitting receipts for payment for goods, which in reality he did not handle. Unless I was born virtuous, without a single crooked bone in my body, I cannot in the world conjure up in my mind a fraud by the shopkeeper. Take as an example the following: The wholesaler delivers to his store 100 dozens of eggs, 100 loaves of bread etc. All of these items are taken out of the store by the shoppers on the same day. Their transactions are entered on the cash register slips. How does he cheat so that he can get away with it? Send to the head office a bill for having handled 1,000 dozen of eggs when the delivery slip indicates that he received only 100dozens? Can anyone be so stupid and a shopkeeper at the same time?

Perhaps the free food staples could be exported to the countries, which do not have such a plan. This is also farfetched. There are stringent import and export regulations of food and plants, dictated by the Departments of Agriculture. Every time you cross the boarder by plane you have to fill out the custom declaration that you do not bring with you any food or plants, and whether what you declare will be for commercial use.

Crossing the boarder by car or by bus, you are asked the same questions. You may smuggle an apple or an orange at a risk of having to pay high fines if caught. Usually you would be instructed to eat them before crossing. Supposedly you ignore all that, rent the refrigerated van and go to the grocery store and download every free food item that you can get. The store closes its doors to the public for the day, being depleted of all the staples. Next you drive to the USA boarder to sell the food to Americans. Can anyone imagine Americans letting you through, with all their sensibility to subsidized goods? It makes more sense to smuggle crack cocaine, tobacco or alcohol, but not perishable foods.

The logistics of smuggling the free food staples south of Canadian boarder (or elsewhere in the world) and converting them into cash is physically impossible. After all, a bag of flour or potatoes is not crack cocaine, which can be hidden in the palm of one's hand and with a single handshake passed on to the buyer, while receiving simultaneous payment in return!

It is also hard to imagine the need for large army of bureaucrats bleeding the system dry. Bureaucrats had their heydays in ancient times, when everything had to be done manually, doing arithmetic in their heads or with the help of abacus. Large number of people were required to find a mistake in bookkeeping. Two auditors getting three different results in their additions had to call the third one to find out who was wrong. Those were also days of job creation, which allowed people to put food on the table, which only governments were experts in, like in the former Soviet Union.

The free food staples plan is nothing more than a nationwide, 24-hours a day, smorgasbord of staples. For a price of $50 a week (this is an arbitrary figure), one would be free to consume to one's heart content (not in a restaurant, of course): bread, flour, milk, cheese, cooking oil, potatoes, etc. The wastage would be factored into food premiums paid. Thus the teenagers would be able to toss half-empty cartons of milk and orange juice in the garbage, have an egg fight using 10 dozen of eggs (hopefully leaving their handguns at home), and yes, the Alitalia flight crew would be able to load their carry-ons with veal, free of charge (provided that veal would be on the staples-menu), and still not ruin the system.

Would there not be a large number of defaulters of the staples premium? The number of people avoiding the payment of food premiums would not be greater than those who are avoiding paying income taxes at the present time. For most recipients of Social Welfare, Old Age Security, Canada pensions, Old Age Supplements, Family Allowances, etc., it would be impossible to default, as their monthly food premium would be deducted at source. The wage earners too would have their food premiums deducted at source in the fashion identical to the deductions of income taxes, union dues, employment insurance and others. The self-employed would have their food premiums deducted from their quarterly income tax installments.

There exists a notion that the Free Food Staples Plan would create an unlimited demand on food through overeating, which would bring difficulties to the supply side, translating into higher costs and controls. However, greed for financial gain and gluttony are not synonymous.

Everyone can imagine unlimited greed to acquire material goods, because the material universe itself is limitless, but not unlimited gluttony. The nature has mercifully built into our bodies controls against gluttony. All humans were given only one stomach of limited capacity, and the reflex to throw up the surplus food to boot. The basic metabolic rate has been constant since our inception, and too many unburned calories convert into fat and smother the body, thus putting an end to the glutton and his gluttony.

There simply could not be a double-digit inflation of food demand, like saying e.g.: "Ten years ago people were satisfied with a quarter-pound-burger, now they demand kilo-burger, and down the road a mega-burger is a distinct possibility, unless the inflationary demand for food be controlled and brought to a halt!"

What about vandalism? This is even harder to visualize. OK! You log to your house 1,000 lbs. of potatoes, 100 dozen eggs, 25 lbs. of flour. What do you do with them? If this is your criminal intent to destroy the system by bilking it dry, you need to hide the evidence, viz. 'to hide the body.' How do you do it? And how do you benefit from it in the end? It would not be cost effective in that you would need to pay for trucking, storage, and the incinerator to get rid of it! A person making e.g. less than $1,000/yr and paying no taxes or premiums would get all staples free of charge. By virtue of his low income he would have no car or no gas to put in the tank. He would be too poor to have his food delivered to his home by a taxicab; and he would be too lazy to log it on his back so that he could later vandalize it. So, how could he abuse the system?

Supposed that he walked to the supermarket and took a shopping cart full of staples and pushed it home. Supposed that he made a second trip and again took more than he needed. How then would he get rid of the surplus? From where would he get the money to pay for extra garbage bags to load the decomposing food unto the curb? Finally, the smell of the vandalized rotting food would point the accusing finger at him as the abuser, unlike what happens in the realm of finance where the embezzlers smell like a rose.

WHERE IS THE MONEY COMING FROM?
WHO WILL PAY?

One can bet one's silk pajamas that, no matter what social project one tried to introduce, the first question uttered in response would be: Where is the money coming from? Who is going to pay for it? In some way it is a silly question. Where is any money in circulation coming from if not from the same circulation, from one pocket into another, from government to people and vice versa?

Some people object to the rule by government, paying taxes, or premiums, and argue that being independent of both and paying as you go would make one feel much freer than if one were a part of the collective. However, we cannot live without taxation because we would not be able to afford all the goods that taxes provide for us. It would be just too expansive.

Taxation is not resented by the super-wealthy, but rather by the vast number of the poor. This fact is exploited in times of elections when the wealthy politicians running for the office frighten the voting public into electing them. They know that without taxes they could not have acquired their wealth. High taxes are essential to organize society in such a way as to enable many people to become obscenely wealthy. After all, one cannot become a multi-millionaire that easy in Burundi or the Republic of Uzbekistan. Taxation, therefore, could be considered as a license to generate profits, or a rental of the social system to individual private enterprises to generate profits. Taxes make the soil arable and ready for the private enterprise to sow and harvest the profits.

Money is printed, of course, to reflect the value of GNP, generated mainly by automation and the silicon chip. Once printed, however, money never gets used up. The same amount of money keeps circulating and is pumped to each individual in form of freebies, interest on money held by the banks, loans to enterprises and back again through the stores to the banks, propelled by trade, greed to make a buck, pressure sales, interest rates, taxation and government's claw-backs.

All money, which we obtain and spend, comes from three sources, as discussed previously: prices, premiums, and taxes. This means that our income comes either from the price we get from selling ourselves, selling something of ourselves, or from selling something belonging to us; or it comes from premiums which insurance companies collect and pay us, subject to contractual agreement or judgment by the courts of law; or from taxes, as when we receive variety of freebies, social assistance, old age security, pensions, food stamps, grants, etc.

In turn, we spend the money thus obtained from these three sources on buying goods contained in the three categories mentioned above: we either pay a price, a premium, or a tax. What differentiates taxes from premium and prices is the degree of our ignorance where our money is going to and for what purposes it will be utilized. We seem to need this knowledge because we feel that we could exercise our vetoes when contemplating giving the consent to the payee how the money paid should be spent. Naturally, all this is nonsense and a self-deception.

The reason for this is simple: whenever we make any purchase, i.e. whenever we spend any money on paying prices, premiums, or taxes, the money changes hands, and we end up with goods and the vendor ends up with money. The money that was 'ours' ceases to be our money and becomes 'his,' the payee's or government's. There will never be a state of affairs when one will either know the fate of our money once it leaves our pocket, or have the power to dictate what the new owner will do with it.

It follows that there could be no such thing as a government or a merchant, wasting our money, for simple reason that it is no longer ours. If my car salesman builds for himself a plush office, installs gilded doorknobs and faucets, supports three mistresses plus lazy, good-for-nothing sons and daughters, and drinks heavy, he doesn't waste *my* money. Do I then go and buy a car elsewhere, even though it is more expensive, and located at inconvenient distance from where I live?

Living in a society is costly. Willy-nilly, one pays for it either by prices, premiums or taxes. There are no free lunches.

Someone has to pay for them. All prices that we pay for food are by definition involuntary. Our stomach holds a gun against our head saying: 'either you put some food in me or you are dead!' Naturally we are free to refuse, but being reasonable people we voluntarily choose to submit. Thus our stomachs always win.

One can refuse to pay for some food items, champagne or Russian caviar for example, but one can never refuse to pay for food staples, because one cannot live without them. Thus it does not make any sense to complain that by being forced to pay premiums for food staples one is forced to pay for something that one would not ordinarily buy.

When one works one pays taxes. A portion of those taxes goes to feed other people beside us. We feed all those who receive social assistance and food-stamps, those who are in the armed forces, in jails and in mental hospitals, homeless, the aged who have no incomes and the very young, the ones stoned on drugs, etc. In addition we feed via humanitarian aid the famished in Ethiopia, Somalia, Bosnia, etc.

It is self-deceptive to believe that if one did not pay any taxes at all that one would feed only oneself and no one else. The truth behind it is this: When I purchase for example a car, vendor has my money and I have his car. What I do with my car is my business, and the vendor has no right to monitor my use of the car, and finding e.g. that I am too destructive in my taking care of it, vowing never to sell me another one. By the same token, I have no business as a purchaser, to keep track of what the vendor does with his money, which before the purchase belonged to me, even if he chooses to feed and support the sloths to which I am violently opposed.

Economy is essentially circulation of money. If circulation of money is stagnant the economy becomes stagnant. Infusion of money revives economy. If the flow of money is cut off the economy is dead. Work itself appears to be inessential for the circulation of money. It is one of the excuses to distribute money. It is a red herring. A good deal of money is earned and distributed without this precondition. Trillions of dollars could be made and wiped out within a week on a stock market without doing any work.

147

As long as we have money we are able to stimulate the economy by making the cash register ring, and no one will quiz us whether we worked for it or not. In a roundabout way, however, without work there would be no goods on the shelf for the consumer to buy, and without it money would stop circulating.

So, how do we fix the circulation of water? Well, we don't. We build dikes, dig irrigation canals, avoid swimming in the shark-infested waters, wear galoshes and carry an umbrella. How do we fix circulation of money? Treat it with all due respect as a volatile, shapeless, fickle and perishable substance. Learn to swim in it without drowning; use it but don't allow ourselves to be used.

The only source of money available to the government is the amount of money already in circulation. Now here is the problem: For the economy to be healthy there has to be vigorous circulation of money. In order to consume the consumer has to have money to spend. If he cannot get it through work the government has to channel it to him in some other form.

Giving welfare is one of such handy excuses. For this reason economy probably needs the poor more than the poor need the economy. But, where does the government find the money? With fewer people working and taxes being unpopular, how can the government maintain a healthy monetary flow to the society at large? Circulation of money (cash flow) is as vital to economy as the circulation of blood is to the humans. Without monetary corpuscles circulating in the body economic it cannot exist. Cut off this circulation and the economy is dead. Restrict it, or slow it down and you produce patchy desertification or economic stagnation. Put too much money into it and the economy goes bust.

Work is not the only modality whereby the money is coming to us. We have plenty of experience in how to bypass work and channel money to each individual, without which the economy would come to a standstill. All of the following examples bypass the requirement of having to work. When we reach the age of 65 we get paid for each year in which we manage to survive. If we are parents we get an allowance for each child until he/she reaches the age of 16. If we worked for 10 -35 years, we get a pension for each year in which we worked. We get paid when we are unemployed, unemployable, poor, sick or disabled. We get money when we suffer injury at work, in a war or in an accident.

With this amount of experience finding new excuses to spread the money around in the next century is a cinch. Here are a few suggestions for a starter: Pay everyone a sum of money for each year of his/her life after the age of 16. Pay an allowance to those who worked 1-9 years. Pay a lifetime gratuity to each person for each year of his/her schooling; more for university education; pay an additional allowance for each certificate, degree and diploma. Pay the doctor, dentist, lawyer, and teacher just for being professionals and leave it up to them to put their knowledge into practice if they want more money.

The freebie that all politicians are promising the electorate, if elected, is "more money in their pockets." This promises to set our economy on the right course. The conventional wisdom states that the more money people have in their pockets the more they spend, which leads to greater demand for consumer goods, and this in turn to more job creation.

If one were to spend only what one had and not one penny more, if one waited until one had the cash for whatever one wanted, one would start hearing the grumbling of Household Finance, the banks, GM Credit Corp and GE Finance, the monetary circulation would be strangulated to a point of collapse, and economy would come to a complete halt.

Can a country afford to feed everyone free of charge? The answer to this question is simple. If under the present food distribution system, for the past number of years, there was no famine in the country it means that no one died of starvation, and that in turn means that everyone had been eating. Since we know that there have not been free lunches, we must accept that those meals were paid for by somebody, somewhere, sometime, no matter from whichever source they came. Whether they came from charities, food banks, garbage cans, they were either paid for directly or else the entire society paid for them collectively in the form of prices, premiums, and taxes.

This means that the food we all have been eating was afforded by the society we lived in. Since it was afforded, it was therefore affordable. The money to pay for all our food was there, collectively in our pockets. What the Free Food Staple Plan would accomplish is this: it would reorganize the total expense of feeding the country in such a way that it could be handled by a single payer. This would make feeding the country more convenient and more economical in addition to dozens of other benefits that would accrue from it.

ROBOTICS

In the future robotics will form a mighty tributary of our present monetary circulation system. The fewer people work the less taxes they would pay and the fewer goods they would buy. It used to be that people's incomes were taxed and then magnanimously a portion of their money was returned to them in the form of a freebie, called a tax rebate, to allow them to have more money in their pockets. However, the human robot appears to be losing his competitive advantage to the artificial one, because he is unfairly taxed.

There is little incentive left for companies to hire human talent. There are lovely tax implications in depreciating equipment. Conversely, there are prohibitive payroll taxes associated with human side. A business owner has no incentive to hire full-time employees and pay all the taxes and disincentives that go with it. He could not be persuaded to change his mind, even if all the prospective employees were highly skilled, experienced and educated.

Reinstitution of slavery, but with a difference, may come to our rescue here. Slavery profited plantation owners when they acquired human robots generated in Africa. This is what slaves were for! Should we be less astute? Let us reintroduce slavery and let us tax them with extreme prejudice, and then spread the benefits amongst all of us!

Aristotle, the Greek philosopher in the fourth century before Christ, the pupil of Plato and the tutor of Alexander the Great, said this of automation (see "Politics"): 'For if every instrument could accomplish its own work, obeying or anticipating the will of others...if, in like manner, the shuttle would weave and the plectrum touch the lyre without a hand to guide them, foremen would *not need labourers*, nor masters slaves.'

Little did Aristotle anticipate that twenty three hundred years later some critics would try to prove him wrong, reasoning that an increased automation required even greater number of slaves and labourers. It is an oxymoronic idea, stating that the more labour labour-saving-devices save the more labour they expend on saving themselves. It is simply not the case.

The robotic slavery may turn out to be our salvation. This is where our future money will be coming from. The taxpayer need not worry. Robots alone may pay for our free staples in the future. Robots, computers, genetically engineered plants, animals, and bacteria will perform all the work. Work by humans, as we know it, is in its last throes of death. A network of automated factories and service stations will be self-supporting, self-generating, and self-repairing. The slave-robots will take care of all our needs, from medical diagnosis and treatment to the haircut and hairstyling.

Robots are the modern equivalents of slaves, as they existed before the abolition of slavery. Our present dilemma is that we allow robots to get away scot-free from paying taxes. Mercifully, computers and robots have no feeling and no intelligence. They cannot be hurt and they are dumb enough to be forced to work day and night with the speed of light and not ask to be fed. Endowed with virtual benefaction they can be made to give up everything they worked for without a whimper.

Here then is the great idea: set up for each virtual worker (representing a robot or a computer) a virtual bank account. Pay each virtual worker a salary or wages based on number of human workers he replaces. Deduct from this salary a premium for his maintenance. Then program this virtual person with virtual benefaction by having him donate all of his earned money to the people of a given country, as if he himself were the human multibillionaire-benefactor. Then have the Board of Directors of The Virtual Benefaction Foundation, set up for this specific purpose, distribute the freebies according to a given formula, e.g.: so much for each year of life after the age of 16, so much for having a degree, so much for pain if there is a history of prior physical or sexual abuse, so much for procreating and raising human robots, etc.

This would seem to me to be a better solution than lowering taxes. For one thing, lower taxes will not work. With fewer people working for lower wages there will be less tax revenues. With lower tax revenues less rebates will reach fewer people. Tax rebate will be of no help to those who pay no taxes to be rebated. The end-result is less money in the pockets of the electorate, less demand for consumer goods, and fewer jobs created.

In practice, every gizmo that does a job, which the human robot used to perform before its introduction, should be taxed to the hilt. Examples follow: answering machines (replacing a receptionist), automatic door opener (replacing a doorman), dish washing machine (dishwasher), bar code scanner (cashier), electronic search engine (librarian), surveillance camera (security guard), alarm systems (policeman), automatic switching devices (a butler), traffic lights (policeman), automatic bank tellers (bank teller), cash machines (bank teller), cigarettes and pop dispensers (convenience store vendor), etc.

The consumer, not having to pay income taxes and sharing the wealth generated by virtual workers, would have more money in his pocket and be able to stimulate the economy. In this fashion, with future 100% unemployment, all the nature (including computers and robotic technology) catering 100% to our needs, we will have regained our Paradise Lost.

PARADISE REGAINED

So, here we are! The food staples, free upon payment of the compulsory food premium, was the magical 'open sesame' command, which ushered in the revolutionary social rebirth. In response to this command the creator relented and, so to say, removed the curse that he had cast upon the soil. In turn, we the creators of robotic workers, cast our spell upon them to work tirelessly day and night and ceaselessly cater to all our whims.

So what does this born-again society look alike under the free food staple plan? On the surface people look healthier, better fed, more contented, relaxed, and less panicky. People appear to be friendlier and less gloomy and paranoid. They appear to be more tolerant of each other. All wolves in sheep's clothing do not threaten to rob anyone of their 'mutton bone.' For this reason one is more likely to be invited for a friendly chat around the table laid with tasty foods.

Going for a walk one notices the absence of beggars and homeless people on the streets. There are fewer overweighed people walking around since they are not confined in their diet to the cheap and fattening types of foods. They eat that which is healthy for them, what their stomachs and not what their pocketbooks dictate to them.

No one is in a great rush, doing his own thing. It is difficult to tell apart the rich from the poor. Money, having lost its fangs and power, is delegated to the lower rank of being just a means of exchange. Consequently, no one stampedes to make a fast buck. There are no strikes and no visible picket lines, no soup kitchens or food banks and no pregnant teenage girls running around.

The air appears to be much cleaner and fresher. At night one is able to see the sky brimming with more stars than one ever had seen before. The green revolution is in full swing; there are more trees around, more parks, and more picnic tables. City traffic is less congested. There are more small stores selling rare specialties and specializing in rare and single items. There are fewer supermarkets, but a profusion of small outlets for the

155

staples. The service is more efficient since one is encouraged to self-serve. There is no opportunity to cheat. Taxes are low. One is able to reach for the stars. Faraway places are that much closer. The world has become smaller.

Newspapers are much thinner, since they do not have to spread the rumours that 'sky is falling.' They do not feature jobseekers' column and there is no talk of unemployment. One immediately notices the absence of chanting of such outworn clichés and slogans as: 'jobs, job, jobs,' 'lower taxes,' 'job creation,' 'inflation,' 'rich getting richer and poor getting poorer,' 'stimulation of economy,' etc.

There is an added specialty channel on television just for the gamblers. There all gambling casinos post all their losses and winnings for the day. Other games of hazard are there too: stock market, bingo, horse races, betting on the outcome of sports events, poker games, etc. Who wants to be a millionaire is also featured; since the winner takes a 25% chance in order to win. Watching the programs on other channels one is spared the agony of being harangued by the value of the dollar, market gains and losses, Dow-Jones averages, Nasdaq composite index, the rate of inflation, the rate of unemployment, and other reports of interest only to the gamesters.

No one is canvassing for cancer, polio, heart and stroke foundation and others, as taxes and health premiums take care of the research in those fields. Drugs are legalized and no one is arrested for drug trafficking or using drugs on prescription. No one is running for political office, as only those who are qualified by virtue of being specialists in their respective fields are selected by other professionals like himself.

The greatest change, however, is the invisible one in the psyche of each individual. Now he is free to make choices, to fashion himself into what he wants to be, where to live, what to study, and what enterprise to undertake. He is free to live his life as it is, as it unfolds itself in time, from moment to moment, ever changing, being an integral part of it, himself forever changing with it.

Thus Paradise Lost becomes transformed into Paradise Regained, and there in the years 2,000, the future man will have found anew his long lost dignity.

The End

BILL OF NO RIGHTS FOR THE THIRD MILLENNIUM*

*We, the sensible people of Earth, in an attempt to assure domestic Tranquility, promote general Welfare, secure the Blessings of Liberty to ourselves and our Posterity, interrupt our fiddling with musical chairs during elections 'while Rome burns,' smooth out the ups and downs of economic depression and inflation, mothball the pre-election slogans of 'jobs, jobs, jobs' and 'lower taxes,' hereby try one more time to ordain and establish common-sense guidelines for our well meaning but misguided brother-keepers, do-gooders, the holders of the ultimate truth, the shepherds of our souls, social engineers, reformers, and religious zealots. We hold these truths to be self-evident, that a whole lot of people are confused by both, **Bill of Rights**, passed by Congress in 1789 as Amendments to the Constitution of the United States, and the **Bill of No Rights** as created by Lewis Napper, a self-described amateur philosopher and professional geek, one day in 1993, and subsequently modified by Rep. Mitchell Kaye.*

*ARTICLE I: You do not have the right to avail yourself of: clean air, potable water, toilet facilities, entrance to parks, roads and highways, education, health care, food, shelter, transportation, clothing, etc., **free** of charge, **unless** these goods and services are collectively prepaid for by taxes and premiums and are declared to be available free of charge to all, for the good of the society, as it has been already accomplished concerning the first six item listed and the seventh one working very well in Canada under a single payer system.*

ARTICLE II: You do not have the right to have a job created for you regardless of race, creed, gender, sexual preferences, religion or employment status, so that you could have the money to buy a new car, big screen TV, and the biggest and fastest computers. It is your responsibility alone to sell yourself, your services, or goods in your possession for a profit, on the free market governed by principles of supply and demand or, if unable, to give up the desire.

ARTICLE III: You do not have the right to dictate to other people how they should treat you, in order to protect you from ever being offended, slighted, angered or otherwise emotionally upset. It is your responsibility to know what hurts you and find out what measures you could take to protect yourself from it and, if unsuccessful, seek professional help.

ARTICLE IV: You do not have the right to demand a guarantee that commercially available tools and products you use, for whatsoever purpose, will cause you no harm, and sue the manufacturer for damages, having been adequately informed about their possible hazards.

ARTICLE V: You do not have the right to demand a compensation for the loss of limb or life if the action you embark upon is willed by you alone, unless such action was forced on you by threats, coercion, intimidation, the law of the country, or socially engineered one-way streets in the gulags of hard work, without there being any exits.

ARTICLE VI: You do not have the right to other people's profits or their wealth of any kind, whether under the guise of increased taxation, or socialist distribution of wealth, in misguided notion that because all people were created equal they were also created to be equal in their wealth.

ARTICLE VII: You do not have the right to demand a second chance in your life to kidnap, rape, torture, maim or kill. The first time around, your crimes were unavoidable because no one, including yourself, knew what you were capable of. Now that you and we know it, your choices are limited to one of the three options available to you, all of which are designed to protect the society from yourself. These options are: 1) Life-long confinement without parole until your death or crippling effect of disease and old age, 2) Suicide (assisted or being allowed to take place by looking the other way), and 3) Release from confinement after surgical treatment designed to permanently disable your power and ability to commit another crime.

ARTICLE VIII: You do not have the right to deny others their right to exist by starving them into employment, productivity or usefulness. Even the three-toed sloth has the right to exist, why not the human couch potato?

ARTICLE IX: You do not have the right to prevent people from organizing themselves in such a way as to prepay for their basic needs consisting of health care, education, food, shelter, transportation, and others, if it is to their advantage, and more economical and convenient.

ARTICLE X: You do not have the right to happiness or the right to define for others what happiness should mean to them. You have only the right to pursue your brand of happiness, unencumbered by the consideration whether this happiness is productive or useful to the society, even if it consists of leading the life of a professional sloth and couch potato, and achieving nothing more than creating another generation of professional sloths and couch potatoes.

ARTICLE XI: You do not have the right to prevent someone from giving a charity or a free ride to whomsoever he wishes, or to force someone to become self-supporting in order that he would refuse to accept or refuse to ask for such a free ride. Whether you choose to do so yourself is entirely up to you.

ARTICLE XII: Money, which you pay for goods and services, ceases to be your money and becomes a profit to the vendor, just as the money, which you receive for selling your goods and services, becomes your profit. You do not have the right to control the vendor's disbursement of his profits and prevent him from supporting a slew of irresponsible, lazy, good for nothing sloths and coach potatoes, who depend on him for their livelihood, as well as other ventures unacceptable to you.

ARTICLE XIII: Every commercial transaction generates profits, and taxation is no exception. Having paid the price to the government, in the form of taxes, for its numerous services to you, you do not have the right to ask the government what it does with the profits derived from the sale of such services. Having received goods and services, you are no more entitled to the refund of money that ceased to be yours the moment you paid your taxes.

ARTICLE XIV: You do not have the power, to prevent a government or anyone else from using its profits to help the poor, weak, old, sick and disabled. However, you have power, but fortunately not the right, to refuse such help to those nearest and dearest to you.

---

* This 'Bill of No Rights for the Third Millennium' was modeled on Lewis Napper's 'Bill of No Rights,' which could be found at http://sandfords.net/Bill_of_No_Rights.htm. It embraces all the principles elucidated in this book.

About The Author

Walter Prytulak was born in Western Ukraine under the Polish rule. He has lived under the dictatorship of several ideologies of -ism: nationalism of Poland, communism of the Soviet Union, fascism of Hitler's Germany, and lastly capitalism of Canada. He is a proponent of a government purged of all clerical and secular ideologies, permitting the private enterprise to function free of its interference. Walter Prytulak is a physician, at present practicing clinical psychiatry in Ontario, Canada.